EXPOSITORY SERMONS ON

GALATIANS

BOOKS BY DR. CRISWELL . . .

Expository Sermons on Revelation – 5 Vols. in 1

Expository Sermons on the Book of Daniel, 4 Vols. in 1

The Bible for Today's World

The Holy Spirit in Today's World

In Defense of the Faith

The Baptism, Filling and Gifts of the Holy Spirit

Expository Sermons on Galatians

Ephesians – An Exposition

Expository Sermons on James

Expository Sermons on the Epistles of Peter

Isaiah — An Exposition

Acts: An Exposition, Volume 1

EXPOSITORY SERMONS ON
GALATIANS

W. A. CRISWELL

ZONDERVAN PUBLISHING HOUSE
OF THE ZONDERVAN CORPORATION
GRAND RAPIDS, MICHIGAN 49506

EXPOSITORY SERMONS ON GALATIANS

Sixth printing 1979
ISBN 0-310-22790-9

Library of Congress Catalog Number 73-13063

Printed in the United States of America

To
the trustees, faculty, and students
of the Criswell Bible Institute

CONTENTS

FOREWORD

The words of Paul preserved in the opening chapter of Galatians still sparkle with the obvious fire and zeal with which they were first penned. The words of this book, a transcript for the most part of expository preaching on the book of Galatians by Dr. W. A. Criswell, still convey some of the fervor and power with which the sermons were originally delivered from the pulpit of the First Baptist Church in Dallas.

Whether the original listener or the reader of this book has come to the understanding that the Scriptures are God-breathed, he finds that when God's message to men is presented with authority and in power, his mind is stimulated and at the same time his soul is warmed and attracted. Men, formed in the image of God, respond to the certainties of God's authoritative and immutable word to them.

Such preaching from Sunday to Sunday and the response it brought from church members and from many of the visitors who are a constant part of each service provided the stimulus for establishing the Criswell Bible Institute in 1970. Its mandate is in-depth Bible teaching, especially in the manner in which that Book has been preached in the First Baptist Church during the pulpit ministry of Dr. Criswell. The pastor serves as the chancellor of the Institute and is a frequent teacher of CBI courses. The Institute has grown to an enrollment of 1,169 part and full-time students, and to a staff of instructors, 15 of whom possess earned doctorates. The growth and vitality of the Institute and the church that sponsors it must be attributed to the blessing of God that falls upon the teaching and preaching and honoring of His inerrant Word.

Through the reading of this book, which is dedicated to those students and teachers, you will sense the power of these truths and possibly a Godward tug to your heart. As Paul wrote, "... I certify you, brethren, that the gospel which was preached by me is not after man. For I neither received it of man, neither was I taught it, but by the revelation of Jesus Christ" (Gal. 1:11, 12). That Gospel sounds a call to which man's soul intuitively responds."

Jack E. Brady
Chairman, Board of Trustees
Criswell Bible Institute

EXPOSITORY SERMONS ON

GALATIANS

Chapter 1

A CHRISTIAN MANIFESTO

Paul, an apostle, (not of men, neither by man, but by Jesus Christ, and God the Father, who raised him from the dead;)

And all the brethren which are with me, unto the churches of Galatia:

Grace be to you and peace from God the Father, and from our Lord Jesus Christ,

Who gave himself for our sins, that he might deliver us from this present evil world, according to the will of God and our Father:

To whom be glory for ever and ever. Amen.

I marvel that ye are so soon removed from him that called you into the grace of Christ unto another gospel:

Which is not another; but there be some that trouble you, and would pervert the gospel of Christ.

But though we, or an angel from heaven, preach any other gospel unto you than that which we have preached unto you, let him be accursed.

As we said before, so say I now again, If any man preach any other gospel unto you than that ye have received, let him be accursed.

For do I now persuade men, or God? or do I seek to please men? for if I yet pleased men, I should not be the servant of Christ.

But I certify you, brethren, that the gospel which was preached of me is not after man.

For I neither received it of man, neither was I taught it, but by the revelation of Jesus Christ.

For ye have heard of my conversation in time past in the Jews' religion, how that beyond measure I persecuted the church of God, and wasted it:

And profited in the Jews' religion above many my equals in mine own nation, being more exceedingly zealous of the traditions of my fathers.

But when it pleased God, who separated me from my mother's womb, and called me by his grace,

To reveal his Son in me, that I might preach him among the heathen; immediately I conferred not with flesh and blood:

Neither went I up to Jerusalem to them which were apostles before me; but I went into Arabia, and returned again unto Damascus.

Then after three years I went up to Jerusalem to see Peter, and abode with him fifteen days.

But other of the apostles saw I none, save James the Lord's brother.

Now the things which I write unto you, behold, before God, I lie not.

Afterwards I came into the regions of Syria and Cilicia;

And was unknown by face unto the churches of Judea which were in Christ:

But they had heard only, That he which persecuted us in times past now preacheth the faith which once he destroyed.

And they glorified God in me. (Gal. 1:1-24)

"Paul, an apostle, (not of men, neither by man, but by Jesus Christ, and God the Father, who raised him from the dead,) and all the brethren which are with me, unto the churches of Galatia" (Gal. 1:1, 2).

Paul addresses his epistle to the churches of Gaul in Asia Minor, not the Gaul of Western Europe. The Galatian churches which were founded and formed by the apostle on his first missionary journey were located in Pisidian Antioch, Iconium, Lystra, Derbe, and possibly other places. The people were Gauls. In the past the great migrations of tribes and nations had been from the east to the west, coming out of central Asia. But in this one instance (after these Gallic people had finally come to the Atlantic, had found the climate inhospitable and in some instances had found the land poor and sterile) they turned back eastward. Migrating in a southeasterly direction, they came to Greece and there were repulsed. They then crossed the Hellespont and overran central Asia Minor, settling there about 280 B.C. In about 180 B.C. they were conquered by the Roman armies, and in 26 B.C. they were organized into the Roman province of Galatia. It is to those Gallic churches that Paul addressed this letter.

who had come out of idolatry. Those Gentiles of Antioch came directly out of paganism into the faith of Christ. They were saved not by keeping a law, not by observing a ceremonial, but by trusting Jesus Christ and Him alone.

Then came Judaistic teachers saying in Antioch, "You cannot be saved by trusting Christ; you must trust Christ *and* keep all the ordinances, ceremonies, and rituals of the law." It created tremendous turmoil and altercation in the church at Antioch. So Paul and Barnabas went to Jerusalem concerning the matter and there met with the apostles in the mother church. In Galatians 2 Paul describes that confrontation in the Jerusalem conference. He says, "And when James [that's the Lord's brother, the pastor of the church at Jerusalem], Cephas [Simon Peter], and John [the sainted apostle John], who seemed to be pillars, perceived the grace that was given unto me, they gave to me and Barnabas the right hands of fellowship, that we should go unto the heathen [Gentiles], and they unto the circumcision [Jews] (v. 9). This is why denominations never bother me because there were denominations from the beginning. It was decided that Peter, James, and John would go to the Jews and they would have a Jewish church, observing Jewish law; whereas Paul and Barnabas would go to the Gentiles and they would have a Gentile church free from the law. And they were compeers, they were equal. Paul was not below James, Cephas, and John, but they were equals. They shook hands in a fellowship in the faith of Christ.

Then Paul goes a step further. He exclaims: "But when Peter was come to Antioch, I withstood him to the face, because he was to be blamed. For before that certain [men] came from James, he did eat with the Gentiles: but when they were come [from Jerusalem], he withdrew and separated himself, fearing them which were of the circumcision" (vv. 11, 12). And Paul says, "I stood Simon Peter to his face, and told him he was acting hypocritically, thus placing upon the Gentiles rules that he himself did not observe, and laws that he himself did not keep." Galatians, indeed, is a polemical letter, full of passion and feeling.

Paul's Defense of His Gospel of Justification by Faith

The second part of the censure of Paul to the Judaizers is

presented in the doctrinal part of the epistle; namely, that we are saved by faith in Christ alone. In the third chapter, when Paul begins the doctrinal position, he says, "Even as Abraham believed God, and it was accounted to him for righteousness" (v. 6). This refers to the fifteenth chapter of the Book of Genesis when Abraham came before God and said: "Lord God, what wilt thou give me, seeing I go childless, and the steward of my house is this Eliezer of Damascus? . . . Behold, to me thou hast given no seed: and, lo, one born in my house is mine heir" (vv. 2, 3). And God took Abraham out under the stars and said, "Look now toward heaven, and tell the stars, if thou be able to number them: and he said unto him, So shall thy seed be" (v. 5). Then the famous verse, "And he [Abraham] believed in the Lord; and he counted it to him for righteousness" (v. 6). That is, Abraham was blessed and rewarded by his trust in the Lord—not by works, not by ceremony, not by ritual—but he was accepted by believing God and by believing in God alone.

As Paul follows the doctrinal argument he writes concerning the keeping of the law, ". . . for it is written [referring to Deut. 4], Cursed is every one that continueth not in all things which are written in the book of the law to do them" (Gal. 3:10). Salvation thus becomes impossible for no man can perfectly keep the law. Paul then adds, "But it is written" [and then Paul quotes from Hab. 2] "The just shall live by faith" (v. 11).

The keeping of the law is like a chain—one does not need to break every one of the links to break the chain. Just break one link and the thing falls. It is thus with the law, Paul avows. One can try to keep all of the laws, but if he breaks only one of them, he is cursed. The Book says so. A man could be saved by keeping the law, but he would have to keep all of it; and when he broke one part of it, immediately he fell into sin and was lost. Therefore, if we are ever saved, we are saved by faith, by trusting Christ, by casting ourselves upon the mercies of God.

No man is justified by the law in the sight of God. No man is good enough to stand before God and say, "I have kept the law perfectly, I am without sin." The apostle avows that "The law was our [paidagogos] (boy's guardian or tutor) to bring us unto Christ, that we might be justified by faith. (v. 24). The purpose of the law was to show us that we are sinners, to reveal to us our lost condition. We have faults, failures, shortcomings and sins before God, doubly revealed to us in the Mosaic legislation. The paidagogos, the school leader, the slave in Roman life who took the child by the hand and led the child to the teacher in the school, is a picture of the law that, Pauls says, leads us to Christ, to confess to Him our shortcomings and our sins. It shows us that we are a dying people, that we cannot save ourselves. If we are ever saved at all, we are saved in the love, mercy, and grace of the blessed Lord Jesus.

Then follows his exhortation and his appeal: "Christ is become of no effect unto you, whosoever of you are justified by the law; ye are fallen from grace" (5:4). The apostle avows in his final appeal, "But God forbid that I should glory [that I should boast], save in the cross of our Lord Jesus Christ, by whom the world is crucified unto me, and I unto the world" (6:14). Truly, one cannot read the epistle nor sense its feeling without all over again reviewing the grace and the mercy that God has given us in the Christian faith. This Book of Galatians is our Magna Carta, our Christian Manifesto of liberty.

When Martin Luther was on his knees climbing up the Scala Sancta before the church of Saint John Lateran in Rome, trying to do penance, seeking to work his way into heaven, trying to find forgiveness of his sins by observing rituals, ceremonies, and law, it was there that the verse from Galatians as from Habakkuk came like a thunderbolt into his soul, "And the just shall live by faith." He walked down those steps, back to Wittenberg, and nailed those ninety-five theses on the door of the church and the Reformation was on! The great thundering instrument in the hands of Martin Luther was this book of Galatians with its text, "The just shall live by faith."

The Ancient and Modern Heresy of Salvation by Works

Today the one great heresy that constantly affects the Gospel of Christ is the Galatians heresy in trying to add something to faith in order that we might be saved, as though the grace of Christ, the cross of Christ, and the blood of Christ alone are not enough to save us. The heresy that one must believe Christ and add something else to the saving Gospel is ever with us and apparently shall be until the consummation of the age. That heresy is expressed in a thousand ways. Here is one: "Belief in Christ is not enough. One must believe and be baptized." Mark's gospel ends at the sixteenth chapter and the eighth verse. Beginning at the ninth verse, some unknown someone tried to finish it. The end of Mark's gospel was lost. When Matthew wrote his gospel, when Luke wrote his gospel, they used Mark, but the end of Mark was lost even when Matthew and Luke were writing. And some unknown, later writer wrote there that heresy, "He that believeth and is baptized shall be saved" (Mark 16:16). Baptism has nothing to do with our salvation. "He that believeth and . . ." then you could add anything: observe the Lord's Supper, pray, read the Bible, kneel—anything. But baptism has nothing to do with being saved. There is no ceremony and there is no rite to be added to the faith of Christ when one is saved. We are saved by Christ alone. And when we add to it, the addition is the Galatian heresy.

The addition of baptism in order to be saved is one example of the heresy. The addition of the Lord's Supper is another. "Believe in the Lord Jesus Christ and observe the Lord's Supper, observe the Mass, and you'll be saved." Or, again, "Believe in the Lord Jesus Christ and live a good life, keep the moral law, and you'll be saved." Or, "Believe in the Lord Jesus Christ and observe Saturday as the Sabbath Day and you'll be saved." The Galatian heresy is over the earth and is prevalent and dominant today. But what is the Gospel? The Gospel according to the revelation in the New Testament, according to the Apostle Paul, and according to the preaching of those first disciples is always this: it is Christ and Christ alone. It is look and live. It is wash and be clean. It is believe and be saved and that alone.

It is look and live: "As Moses lifted up the serpent in the wilderness, even so must the Son of man be lifted up: That whosoever believeth in him should not perish, but have eternal life" (John 3:14, 15). It is wash and be saved and be clean and be white: "These are they which came out of great tribulation, and have washed their robes, and made them white in the blood of the Lamb" (Rev. 7:14). It is believe and be saved: "... What must I do to be saved? ... Believe on the Lord Jesus Christ, and thou shalt be saved ..." (Acts 16:30b, 31). Always our salvation is in Christ. "The just shall live by faith." "And he believed God and it was accounted unto him for righteousness." We are saved by Christ alone and not by Christ and something else.

Three Avowals From Scripture of Salvation in Christ Alone

Let me make three avowals concerning the divine truth that we are saved by Christ alone. One, our salvation is always personal and not legalistic, ceremonial, or ritualistic. It is always and ever personal. We are saved not by a code, not by a law, not by a set of rituals or ceremonies, not by observing days or times, but we are saved by our personal relationship with Jesus Christ. It is *He* who saves us and *He* alone. Such a personal relationship is beautifully illustrated in human life and experience. When a man falls in love, the whole tenor of his life becomes something else. He seeks to please that someone whom he loves, to do things for the love of his life, to be cognizant of her wishes and desires. Becoming a Christian is exactly like that—one has fallen in love with Christ. And the whole issue of his life thereafter flows toward Him—praying to Him, loving Him, walking with Him, giving one's life to Him, hoping in Him, dying in Him, trusting in Him, believing in Him, now and in the hour of death and in the judgment that is to come. It is a personal relationship when one is saved by loving, believing, and trusting Christ. Salvation always is personal. It is never legalistic. It is never ceremonial.

Second, our salvation is always inward and not outward. It is of God and not of men. Many times I am asked, "Why do you have these children come to the front of the church twice during the invitation?" The answer is plain: it is easy for a child to get the idea that he becomes a Christian by joining the church, that he becomes a Christian by being baptized. Most young children will get that idea. They think they are saved by joining the church. A child is asked to come forward twice, first, in order to confess his faith in the Lord Jesus; this is, accepting Christ as his Savior. This is something that no one else can do for him. It has to happen in his heart. The child is saved by trusting Jesus in his heart. Jesus forgives his sins. He regenerates the child through His Holy Spirit. He writes the born-again believer's name in the Book of Life. Trusting Jesus is an inner experience between the child and God. Christ alone can do that—that is what it is to confess one's faith in the Lord.

The child is asked to come forward the second time, after a period of training, in order for the church to accept the child as a candidate for baptism and thereafter as a member of the church. The pastor can baptize the child into the household of faith, but that is not salvation. Conversion is something different. It is in an altogether different world. It is only *after* conversion that we are to be baptized into the fellowship of the church. One can be a member of the church and be lost. One can be a Sunday school teacher and be lost. One can be a deacon and be lost. One can be a member of the church ever since he was born and be lost. Before we join the church we must be saved. That is something only God can do for us. The experience is inward and not outward. There is not anything a man can do for me that saves me. Regeneration is something that God does for my heart. It is personal, not legalistic, nor ceremonial. It is inward and not outward, it is of God and not of man, something God has to do that a man cannot do.

Third, it is spiritual and not material. It is of faith and of promise. It is looking to God. "While we look not at the things that are seen, but at the things which are not seen: for the things which are seen are temporal; but the things which are not seen are eternal" (2 Cor. 4:18). It is spiritual, it is inward, it is upward, it is Godward; it is not outward, it is not materialistic, legalistic, or of man. It is of faith and promise.

When I began preaching at seventeen years of age, I listened to those marvelous experiences that people proclaimed to have had in the Lord. They saw balls of fire from heaven, they saw lights, they saw angels from heaven. I had no experience like that. I was saved as a ten-year-old boy. As I listened to those unusual testimonies, I concluded that I was not born again. I was not saved. I was not regenerated. When I was a boy beginning to preach, on Sundays I would preach in my little church, then every night during the week I would get down by the side of my bed and cry unto God, saying: "O God, I am not saved. I am not really born again. I am not a Christian, actually, for I have not seen a light, I have not seen an angel, and I have not seen a ball of fire from heaven." Those were the most agonizing days in the world. All I had done as a ten-year-old boy was in faith accept Jesus as my Savior, and with many tears I went down to the front of the church and gave my hand to the pastor, told him that I had given my heart to God and asked that I might be baptized and become a member of the church. That is the way I was saved—just by trusting in the Lord. And then as I listened to those testimonies I concluded: "Why, that is not enough. I have to see an angel."

As I read, as I prayed, as I studied, oh, the revelation that came to me from God's Book. Never an angel. Never a light. Never a ball of fire. Never! I am saved by accepting the Lord, by trusting in Jesus, His Word and His promise. And the verse that sustained me then and to which I cling now is John 1:12, "But as many as received him, to them gave he power to become the sons of God, even to them that believe on his name." And that verse never changes. I can awaken at two o'clock in the morning and there it is. In youth, in manhood, and in old age, there it is. I am saved by trusting Christ alone. Why, my brethren, if I were to see an angel today, if I were to see a light from heaven, if I were to see a ball of fire from the sky, it would never occur to me now to connect it, to identify it, to make it an addendum to my salvation. For I am saved by trusting in the Lord and in Him alone. I am saved by believing the promises of God and by casting myself upon the mercies of Christ. When I do that I am saved. "For whosoever shall call upon the name of the Lord shall be saved." "The just shall live by faith." Just trust Him.

So I go on not knowing.
I would not know if I might.
I would rather walk with Christ by faith
Than to walk by myself with sight.

I had rather walk with Him in the dark
Than to walk alone in the light.

That is what it is to be a Christian. That is what Paul wrote to the churches of Galatia and that is the same Gospel when a man preaches it today. It is not Christ and good works, it is not Christ and a ceremony, it is not Christ and a ritual, it is not Christ and the observance of the Lord's Supper or the observance of days or seasons. It is not Christ *and anything.* It is *Christ alone!* It is He who saves us. "For by grace are ye saved through faith." It is of Him and Him alone. And when a man gets to heaven he is not going to say up there in glory, "Here I am . . . saved by Christ *and* good works, or saved by the Lord *and* by the ministries of some pastor," however sanctified and holy he may be. No! When we get to heaven, this is what we are going to sing, "Unto him who loved us and washed us from our sins in his own blood . . . to Him be glory and dominion for ever and ever. Amen" (Rev. 1:5, 6).

Saved by the blood of the Crucified One!
All hail to the Father, all hail to the Son,
All hail to the Spirit, the great Three in One!
Saved by the blood of the Crucified One!

This is our Galatian manifesto of liberty in Christ.

Chapter 2

THE ONLY GOSPEL

> I marvel that ye are so soon removed from him that called you into the grace of Christ unto another gospel:
>
> Which is not another; but there be some that trouble you, and would pervert the gospel of Christ.
>
> But though we, or an angel from heaven, preach any other gospel unto you than that which we have preached unto you, let him be accursed.
>
> As we said before, so say I now again, If any man preach any other gospel unto you than that ye have received, let him be accursed. (Gal. 1:6-9)

This message is a sermon on dogmatism, on finality, on authoritarianism, which is an unusual message to hear today in the midst of our studied broad-minded liberalism. The very tone of the text is antithetical to everything that men are taught in the academic world. Let us read again the text from Galatians 1:6-12.

> I marvel that ye are so soon removed from him that called you into the grace of Christ unto another gospel: Which is not another; but there be some that trouble you, and would pervert the gospel of Christ. But though we, or an angel from heaven, preach any other gospel unto you than that which we have preached unto you, let him be accursed. As we said before, so say I now again, If any man preach any other gospel unto you than that ye have received, let him be accursed. For do I now persuade men, or God? or do I seek to please men? for if I yet pleased men, I should not be the servant of Christ. But I certify you, brethren, that the gospel which was preached of me is not after man. For I neither received it of man, neither was I taught it, but by the revelation of Jesus Christ.

Is not that strange? "But though we, or an angel from heaven, preach any other gospel unto you than that which we have preached unto you, let him be accursed." In the Greek the language is *anathama esto* with emphasis on *anathama*, literally meaning "let him be devoted to destruction, let him be damned, let him be accursed."

And then as though that were not enough, Paul says it again. "As we said before, so say I now again, If any man preach any other gospel unto you than that ye have received, *anathama esto*." "Let him be accursed, devoted unto destruction." *Esto*, "let him be." Ah, it is a different world when one looks at the Book and when one looks at the present liberal, eclectic inclusiveness. Our generation is not to believe anything, not really. Today one certainly is not to be dogmatic about anything. We are to be latitudinarian. If one wishes in modern society, and especially in academic circles, to present the image of being narrow-minded and provincial, then believe something—have conviction about something. "Here I stand, so help me God, I can do no other." Such a Martin Luther sentiment today is absolutely and altogether *out*.

We are taught not to reach any final conclusion but to keep our minds "open," and by that these liberal thinkers mean for us not to believe anything with finality. Let everything remain in solution, in limbo.

The Inevitable Accompaniments of So-called Broad-mindedness

Let me point out three things that follow that so-called broad-minded anti-provincialism. First, when one per se takes the position of broad-mindedness, it carries with it an innate and congenital accompaniment that speaks of cheap shallowness, like a river that is three miles broad and three inches deep. The only difference between a swamp and a river is that one has banks and runs in a channel, and one is broad and spreads itself all over. It is possible to be so without conviction that men are as spineless as though they were jellyfishes—without backbone, without strength, without "morphus," without form at all. There was a broad-minded, liberal minister who resigned, and after his announced resignation one of his parishioners came up to him and said, "Oh, how we feel the loss in your leaving." He added, "You know, before you came, I cared not for God nor man nor the devil, but under your fine preaching I have come to love all three!"

The first result of this broad-minded, convictionless attitude and spirit is that men become cheap and shallow. The second accompaniment is that men become so anemic, so without iron and strength, that they find themselves incapable of opposing even an undisguised enemy. Anything can sweep them away, mold them into something else. In reading the Bible, I often think of those dedicated believers in the first Christian centuriės who laid down their lives for the faith. Conviction and persuasion was so deep in them that they faced lions rather than give up an iota of their commitment to Christ. They suffered to death. Then men did not make the doctrine, but the doctrine (revealed from heaven, according to the Apostle Paul) made the men. Strength, conviction, power lay in the faith. They believed something unto death, and they sealed it with their life-blood.

A third thing that always follows this broad, liberal, latitudinarianism (to believe nothing in particular) is the language of these "Christianettes." Their sentimental attitudes and their soft, inclusive pronouncements ultimately destroy the faith itself. I personally have never met a liberal who was not affable, congenial. He does not believe anything in particular, why should he object to anything? Why should he speak out against anything? His broad-mindedness includes anything and everything. But he drowns the faith in his honeyed words. A practical illustration of that appears in the life of the famous French philosopher, Renan. He was educated to be a minister. He was a professor in a theological school. He was a skeptic of skeptics, yet he had such a romantic and dramtic attitude about Jesus that I have even quoted him in some of my own sermons. The things he would say were unusually superlative. But notice this observation. Dr. Pressence said of Renan: "Renan very skillfully undermines Christianity while profuse in its praise; he buries it in flowers. He comes to the tomb of the Saviour not to weep and worship like the women of the Gospel, but to stifle with perfumes and spices any lingering spark of life in the religion of Jesus. He does not deal a blow with a sharp sword; no, he embalms. But the result is the same as though he had made a violent attack." It is possible, literally, to destroy the Christian faith in sweetness, in perfume, and in broad-mindedness, convictionless liberalism.

The Early Christians Died for an Uncompromised Faith

The Christian faith is of all things and first of all authoritarian. It is non-compromising. It is absolute and final. It is that or nothing at all. The Roman Empire did not demand of those early Christians whom they fed to the lions, whom they burned at the stake, whom they plunged into boiling caldrons of oil, whom they crucified—the Roman Empire did not ask that they give up their faith in Christ nor that they cease attending churches nor do anything whereby they would separate themselves from their Lord. The Roman Empire was of all things broad-minded in its religious policies. When they conquered a nation they accepted that nation's god. They brought the god to Rome and put him in the Pantheon with all the rest of the gods they had previously collected. One of the secrets of the success of the building of the Roman Empire was that tolerant attitude toward the religions of the provinces. It made no difference to the Romans. They allowed all of the gods to be worshiped. If one liked Neptune, there he is. If he liked Osiris, there he is. If he liked Isis, there she is; or Venus, there she is; or Diana, there she is; or Jove, there he is; or Juno, there she is. One could worship any god that he pleased. As time went on, the leaders of Rome began to see that they needed some kind of a faith, some kind of a religion to put cohesiveness in the empire, to hold it together. They found that hope of a common religion in the worship of the emperor. Wherever there were these shrines to the gods, there would also be along with them a shrine to the emperor. Men could worship all the gods they pleased, but they were also asked to bow before the image of the emperor.

Now the Christian was asked to do obeisance before the shrine of the Caesar. How was he asked to show his allegiance to the emperor and the empire? In a little, simple act that one would think would be nothing at all. As a matter of patriotism, as a matter of loyalty to the government, the Christian was asked to take a little pinch of incense and put it on the altar fire that burned before the image of the emperor. The disciple of Christ was asked to do this as an act of loyalty and patriotism to the government. But the first-century Christian refused to do it! When Polycarp, the pastor of the martyr church at Smyrna, was burned at the stake, the judge asked him to place a pinch of incense on the flame that burned before the altar of the image of the emperor. If the pastor would do this, the judge would spare his life. Polycarp refused and died because of that refusal.

There was a vast, deep unusualness about the persecution of the Christians in the Roman Empire. It was a new thing for Rome to persecute in the name of God or religion. But the Caesars persecuted the Christians because they refused any other faith, any other act of worship except before Jesus Christ, Jesus the Lord. Now that is the kind of finality and non-compromising authoritarianism that made the Christian faith. The Christian faith is of all things dogmatic. It is that or it is nothing at all. I speak of it in three categories: first, in the finality of Christ; second, in the finality of the Book; and third, in the finality of its way of salvation. There is room for none other.

The Finality of Christ

First, in the finality of Christ, the dogmatic manner and spirit of our Lord. "Dogmatism" is an evil word today, and when I place it with our Savior, it may sound strange, but if I am true to the Bible I cannot but speak of the dogmatism of Jesus. He never comes forward with a series of opinions, and then let His hearers choose which one he might like. The Lord never sends out diametrically opposite theories, and then lets you choose whichever you please. When the Lord speaks, He never speaks comparatively. He always speaks powerfully and absolutely. His words are always superlative. They are not an exposition, but are the text itself. For example, in Matthew, in the Sermon on the Mount, we find, "Ye have heard that it hath been said, An eye for an eye, and a tooth for a tooth: But I say unto you, That ye resist not evil: but whosoever shall smite thee on thy right cheek, turn to him the other also. And if any man will sue thee at the law, and take away thy coat, let him have thy cloak also. And whosoever shall compel thee to go a mile, go with him twain" (Matt. 5:38-41), "... when Jesus had ended these sayings, the people were astonished at his doctrine: For he taught them as one having authority, and not as the scribes" (Matt. 7:28, 29).

Another instance of the absolute authority of Jesus appears in Matthew 8. "And when Jesus was entered into Capernaum, there came unto him a centurion, beseeching him, and saying, Lord, my servant lieth at home sick of the palsy, grievously tormented. And Jesus saith unto him, I will come and heal him. The centurion answered and said, Lord, I am not worthy that thou shouldest come under my roof: but speak the word only, and my servant shall be healed. For I am a man under authority, having soldiers under me: and I say to this man, Go, and he goeth; and to another, Come, and he cometh; and to my servant, Do this, and he doeth it. When Jesus heard it, he marvelled, and said to them that followed, Verily I say unto you, I have not found so great faith, no, not in Israel" (vv. 5-10). The finality of Christ! All authority is in His hands. The Lord said, "You go your way, your servant is healed." And he was healed from that very hour. That is the Lord.

Another example of the finality of the words of Jesus is found in the seventeenth chapter of the gospel of Matthew. On top of the Mount of Transfiguration, when Peter saw Elijah and Moses on either side of the Lord, the apostle said, "Lord, it is good for us to be here: if thou wilt, let us make here three tabernacles [three booths used in the time of the Feast of the Tabernacles]; one for thee, and one for Moses, and one for Elias [Elijah]. While he yet spake, behold, a bright cloud overhadowed them: and behold a voice out of the cloud, which said, This is my beloved Son, in whom I am well pleased; hear ye him" (vv. 4, 5). Hear Him! His words are final, absolute, and authoritarian. Listen to these verses of the poet:

Hushed be the noise and strife of the schools,
Volume and pamphlet, sermon and speech;
The lips of the wise and the prattle of fools;
Let the Son of Man teach!

Who has the key to the future but He?
Who can unravel the knots of the skein?
We have groaned and have travailed and sought to be free:
We have travailed in vain.

Bewildered, dejected, and prone to despair,
To him as at first do we turn and beseech:
"Our ears are all open! Give heed to our prayer!
O, Son of Man, teach!"

O Lord Jesus, tell us what to do, what to believe. Reveal to us the mind and wisdom of God. Do it, Lord!

Dogmatic, authoritarian, and severe is the blessed Jesus, this Jesus who took little babes in His arms and blessed them, the gentle Jesus who said: "Come unto me, all ye that labour and are heavy laden, and I will give you rest. Take my yoke upon you, and learn of me: for I am meek and lowly in heart: and ye shall find rest unto your souls" (Matt. 11:28, 29). In Matthew 23, one can see His ringing, bitter denunciation of the scribes and Pharisees. "You hypocrites, you whited sepulchres, you are full of dead men's bones—you shall receive a greater damnation, you generation of vipers of snakes!" (cf. Matt. 23:27, 33). That is the same Lord Jesus. Listen to Him again as He speaks of the powers of hell. Practically all that we know about hell comes from the lips of our Lord. Oh, the severity of Christ!

Let us look at another instance of the uncompromising demands of Christ in the gospel of Mark. "... There came one running, and kneeled to him.... Then Jesus beholding him loved him" (Mark 10:17, 21). This rich young ruler had kept all the commandments from his youth up. "What lack I yet?" And the Lord said to him: "You are a rich man, and your riches divide you from God. Your heart is where your treasure is in this world, in what you have. Get rid of it. Sell everything you have and give it away. Come, follow me" (cf. Mark 10: 20, 21). The young man *stugnazo*. Twice is the word *stugnazo* used in the Bible. One instance is when the Lord said that when you see the sky red and *stugnazo*, "lowering," the clouds, boiling, it signifies certain kinds of weather. The other place it is used is describing the face of that rich young ruler—*stugnazo*. The war in his soul was registered in his face, in his countenance. "And he was sad at that saying, and went away grieved" (Mark 10:22). Why did not the Lord say to him as he walked away: "Young man, come back. Do not go away like that. Let us talk about this. Maybe we can soften the blow. Maybe we can compromise. Maybe we can work out some details. Come back. Do not go away." Did the Lord do that? No. He watched the young man go away. He never lessened the demand, never. The finality of the demeanor and manner of the Lord Himself is like that—uncompromising. Tender, precious, He laid down His life for us, but He never lowered the standards of His appeal.

The Finality of the Holy Scriptures

We speak now of the finality of the Book, the Word of God. Jesus introduces without apology proofs from the Word of God. What the Holy Scriptures said was to Him the ultimate and final authority. He said, "It is written," as He faced the devil-tempter in Matthew 4:4 "It is written" He said in Matthew 11:10 when men objected to His ministry. "It is written" He said in Matthew 26:24 when He was betrayed by Judas. "It is written" He said in Luke 24:46 when He taught His disciples the meaning of His death and crucifixion.

This attitude toward the inspired Scriptures is evident throughout the teaching ministry of our Lord. Let us read again Matthew 22:29; "Jesus answered and said unto them, Ye do err, not knowing the scriptures, nor the power of God." John 5:39 says, "Search the scriptures; for in them ye think ye have eternal life: and they are they which testify of me." In John 6:63 we read, "It is the spirit that quickeneth; the flesh profiteth nothing: the words that I speak unto you, they are spirit, and they are life." And John 15:3 says, "Now ye are clean through the word which I have spoken unto you."

Both the Old Testament and the New Testament convey this same deep persuasion that the written testimony is the final revelation of God Himself and as such is binding and authoritative. The prophet Isaiah wrote, "To the law and to the testimony: if they speak not according to this word, it is because there is no light in them" (Isa. 8:20). And the sainted Apostle John closes the Apocalypse with these somber words: "For I testify unto every man that heareth the words of the prophecy of this book, If any man shall add unto these things, God shall add unto him the plagues that are written in this book: And if any man shall take away from the words of the book of this prophecy, God shall take away his part out of the book of life, and out of the holy city, and from the things which are written in this book" (Rev. 22:18, 19).

There is no mistaking the clear, resounding testimony of the Word of God to itself as being forever authoritarian, ultimate, and final.

The Finality of the Gospel Way of Salvation

We speak last of the finality of the Gospel way of salvation. How many ways of salvation are there? How many of these roads that the broad-minded speak of lead finally to God and to heaven? There are uncountable ways to be saved, they avow. They are as numerous as the individual speculations of the people who hold to them, they say. Does the Bible say that? Listen to the words of Christ Himself: "Verily, verily, I say unto you, He that entered not by the door into the sheepfold, but climbeth up some other way, the same is a thief and a robber . . . I am the door: by me if any man enter in, he shall be saved, and shall go in and out, and find pasture" (John 10:1, 9). There is one door. There is one way. And there are no other ways. There is one way and that is in Christ. "Neither is there salvation in any other, for there is no other name under heaven given among men, whereby we must be saved" (Acts 4:12). Listen again to the sainted John as he writes in the closing words of his first epistle: "He that believeth on the Son of God hath the witness in himself: he that believeth not God hath made him a liar; because he believeth not the record that God gave of his Son. And this is the record, that God hath given to us eternal life, and this life is in his Son. He that hath the Son hath life; and he that hath not the Son of God hath not life" (1 John 5:10-12). Plainly, authoritatively, and finally stated, it is this simple: If a man is to be saved, he must be saved in Christ.

Ah, how these words make me tremble, make me bow, make me pray, make me look up to heaven, make me plead for grace and mercy and help from God! The revelation of the Lord is not double-faced nor is it deceptively speculative. It is not as though we were selecting opinions. It is not as though we were in dilemmas choosing theories. It is not as though we were listening to blind, metaphysical gropings. The sound of the trumpet is clear in the Word of God. It is final. It is superlative, never comparative. The authoritarianism of the Gospel! "My brethren, though I or an angel from heaven preach any other gospel unto you than ye have heard, *anathama esto*. Let him be accursed." One faith, one Lord, one baptism, one God and Father for us all, one Book, one way—just one!

CHAPTER 3

THE FAITH HE ONCE DESTROYED

> For ye have heard of my conversation in time past in the Jews' religion, how that beyond measure I persectued the church of God, and wasted it:
>
> And profited in the Jews' religion above many my equals in mine own nation, being more exceedingly zealous of the traditions of my fathers.
>
> But when it pleased God, who separated me from my mother's womb, and called me by his grace,
>
> To reveal his Son in me, that I might preach him among the heathen; immediately I conferred not with flesh and blood:
>
> Neither went I up to Jerusalem to them which were apostles before me; but I went into Arabia, and returned again unto Damascus.
>
> Then after three years I went up to Jerusalem to see Peter, and abode with him fifteen days.
>
> But other of the apostles saw I none, save James the Lord's brother.
>
> Now the things which I write unto you, behold, before God, I lie not.
>
> Afterwards I came into the regions of Syria and Cilicia:
>
> And was unknown by face unto the churches of Judaea which were in Christ:
>
> But they had heard only, That he which persecuted us in times past now preacheth the faith which once he destroyed.
>
> And they glorified God in me. (Gal. 1:13-24)

The tone of the Galatian letter is very polemical, and the reason for it is no less plain. There were ceremonial teachers who were trying to destroy the faith of the churches Paul had founded in the Roman province of Galatia. They were teaching new converts that one cannot be saved by trusting Christ alone, but one must also add to that faith certain ceremonial rituals, rites, and obediences of the law.

These Judaizers dogged Paul's steps wherever he went—in Syria, in Antioch, in Cilicia, and finally in those churches he had founded on his missionary journey. It was the battle of Acts 15 all over again, when the council of God's people gathered in the Holy City to make a decision concerning whether or not one could be saved just by trusting Christ or whether he must add to that faith certain rites, ceremonies, and kept commandments.

The attack of the Judaizing enemies of Paul was centered against him personally. They said he was not a real and actual apostle but rather a false apostle. He was not one of the original Twelve. He never saw the Lord in the days of His flesh, nor did he receive a commission from the original Twelve. They claimed that Paul's message was not authentic since it did not come from Christ nor did he walk in the tradition of the original apostles. Thus they attacked Paul personally. The letter to the Galatians is in answer to that attack, both against the Gospel he preached (the message that heaven had revealed to him personally), and the authenticity of his apostleship.

One might think that when the apostle writes he would be apologetic. It was certainly true that he was not one of the Twelve. It was vividly true that he was separate and apart from the original apostles who followed the Lord in His Galilean, Judaean, and Perean ministries. But instead of Paul being sychophantic or defensive, you find in his letter no extenuation. There is no rationalization. Rather, he seems eagerly willing to maintain his separate call and his unique apostleship. He does it with zeal, with temerity, and with great boldness.

The Three Avowals Paul Makes Concerning Himself

Paul avows of himself three things: first, that his call is independent; second, that his gospel is independent; and third, that his work is independent. There was no hierarchy, there was no man, there was no church, there was no anyone of flesh and blood who had anything to do with him and his ministry for Christ. He stands boldly alone, uniquely the apostle by revelation. He avows that position in the first sentence of his letter, "Paul, an apostle, (not of men, neither by man, but by Jesus Christ, and God the Father, who raised him from the dead)."

Sometimes in reading the Bible I wonder about the apostle who was chosen to take the place of Judas. In the first chapter of the Book of Acts, the apostles and the brethren met together. This chronology is before Pentecost, before the Holy Spirit was poured out. They nominated two men for that apostleship, and the lot fell upon Matthias who was numbered with the eleven. I have ofen wondered if he were not man's choice—the choice of flesh and blood. But the real apostle who was chosen to take the place of Judas is the Apostle Paul, Saul of Tarsus, to whom the Lord Jesus appeared on the road to Damascus. Certainly that call was from heaven. It was independent of man. It came from God.

The Gospel According to Paul, a Fifth Gospel

Not only is the call of the apostle independent, but his gospel is independent. It is actually a fifth gospel. It comes uniquely, separately, and apart from the tradition of the apostles who followed the Lord in the days of His earthly ministry. Paul writes: "I certify you, brethren that the gospel which was preached of me is not after man, it is not by tradition, nor am I repeating things that I have heard from Peter and John. Nor am I saying things that I learned in the church, but the gospel which I preach unto you is not after man for I neither received it of men, neither was I taught it by men, but by direct revelation of Jesus Christ" (c. Gal. 1:11, 12).

The apostles, the original Twelve, followed the Lord around Judaea, Samaria, Perea, and Galilee for three years. They sat at the feet of Jesus. But when the Apostle Paul was called, he went to Arabia and then to Damascus for three years where he was taught by direct revelation from God the gospel that he preached. It is a fifth gospel. It is unique, separate, and apart. He avows that he received it by direct revelation from Christ in heaven. One can see the uniqueness of the gospel of Paul in comparing his message and where he learned it with that of Dr. Luke. When Paul was in prison in Caesarea for over two years, his companion, Luke, was with him. Luke went to see Mary, the mother of Jesus. He talked to her and to all of the eyewitnesses of Christ's ministry. In the beginning verses of the gospel of Luke, the doctor states that he obtained documents depicting the work of our Lord. Thus he studied along with the notes he made as he listened, talked, and visited with those early followers of Christ. This companion of Paul then wrote down in the gospel of Luke these things that he had heard, seen, and read. Luke's gospel is from the eyewitnesses and from the documents of the day in which he lived.

In contradistinction to the manner in which Luke received his gospel, the Apostle Paul says that the gospel that he preached he received not from the mouths of men, not from the tradition of the apostles, not from the witnesses of the church, but he received it by direct revelation from heaven. It is an independent message. It is a fifth gospel tradition. It is separate and uniquely set apart. In that gospel of Paul there are astonishing revelations. He was in Paradise, the third heaven. He heard things unutterable. Paul speaks of the dissolution of this earthly tabernacle, of the time and order of the resurrection from the dead, of the return of our Lord, and of the rapture of the Church. All of these glorious disclosures that are revealed in the gospel writings of Paul cause his message to be marvelously independent. The revelations came not from man but they came from heaven itself, directly from Christ in glory.

The Independent Work of the Apostle Paul

Not only was his call independent, and not only was his message—his gospel—independent, separate from the Twelve, but the work that he did was an independent work. Compare Romans 15:18-21: "For I will not dare to speak of any of those things which Christ hath not wrought by me, to make the Gentiles obedient, by word and deed, through mighty signs and wonders, by the power of the Spirit of God; so that from Jerusalem, and round about unto Illyricum, I have fully preached the gospel of Christ. Yea, so have I strived to preach the gospel, not where Christ was named, lest I should build upon another man's foundation. But as it is written, To whom he was not spoken of, they shall see: and they that have not heard shall understand." His ministry flowed in no wise in the channel and in the form and pattern of the original Twelve. For example, the Apostle Paul will write: "For I am the least of the apostles, that am not meet to be called an apostle, because I persecuted the church of God. But by the grace of God I am what I am: and his grace which was bestowed upon me was not in vain; but I laboured more abundantly than they all: yet not I, but the grace of God which was with me" (1 Cor. 15:9, 10). "I labored more abundantly than they all." Were the disciples called Christians first in Jerusalem? No. In Judea? No. In Saramia? No. In Galilee? No. Where were the disciples first called Christians? They were called Christians first under the ministry of the Apostle Paul in Antioch.

In the Council of Jerusalem (Acts 15 and Gal. 2) it was decided that Peter, James (the Lord's brother) and John would go to the circumcision. That is, they would follow the tradition of the Jewish people. They would worship in the Temple and keep the Jewish law. They created what later became known as an Ebionitic church, a Hebrew church. Had that been the whole of the Christian faith, it would have perished under the rubble and the debris of the walls of Jerusalem when the city was destroyed in A.D. 70. The Ebionitic sect of the Christian faith died out completely. But the assignment given to the Apostle Paul and to Barnabas in Acts 15 and in Galatian 2 in the Council of Jerusalem was that they should go to the Gentiles. Thus the independent ministry of the work of the Apostle Paul covered the civilized world. It is the type of Christian faith and the Christian message that we know today. The work of Paul was expansive. He was sent by the Lord to the Gentiles. "But when it pleased God, who separated me from my mothers' womb, and called me by his grace, To reveal his Son in me, that I might preach him among the heathen . . ." (Gal. 1:15, 16). And it is that set-apart stream of the Christian faith that we know, that we receive, and that we follow today.

The Sovereign, Elective Purpose of God

Now, let me expatiate just for a moment on Paul's own categorizing of this call and message that he received from

God. Do you notice that he says it was from his "mother's womb," it pleased God to prepare him for his heavenly ministry? His calling was not an afterthought of the Almighty, but when he was conceived, God's purposes were in mind for his vast missionary work. The apostle writes so often of this divine choice, this sovereign election in the lives of men. In Romans 9, for example, Paul will discuss the election of Jacob—of Israel. In the womb of Rebecca, he says, there were two boys—twins. One was named Esau and one was named Jacob, and before they were born the Lord chose Jacob and said the elder, Esau, shall serve the younger. The sovereign, elect purposes of God were planned before the children were born. A like revelation is recorded in Jeremiah 1. Jeremiah repeats the word of the Lord that God had called him from the time of his birth, that God had formed him in his mother's womb for his prophetic ministry. The same sovereignty is illustrated again in Luke 1 when the angel Gabriel said that the child (later called John the Baptist) should be filled with the Holy Spirit from his mother's womb. And thus it is in the life of the Apostle Paul. When he was born, God formed him for the missionary work he was to do.

Am I, therefore, to believe that when God makes us and creates us in the secret parts of our mother's body, He does that for a reason and for a purpose—that God has an elected choice and program and plan for our lives? If I can understand the Bible at all, it is just that. When you were conceived, when you were formed, when God gave you a soul and breathed into your body the breath of life, God also had at that time a plan and a purpose for you. Paul speaks of his calling as being from his mother's womb. His apostleship was not something that hapepned as an afterthought. It was not something that developed in life, but it was from the beginning the sovereign and elect purpose of the almighty God.

As Saul of Tarsus he had superior, excellent training. He said to the Roman centurion, "I am a citizen of no mean city," referring to Tarsus, the capital of the Roman province of Cilicia. Almost certainly Paul attended the Greek university there. He was conversant with Greek language, literature, and poetry. But he was also a Hebrew of the Hebrews. He was taught by Gamaliel, the great rabbi in Jerusalem. He was brought up in the tradition of the Jewish faith, and was zealous in it. He was a Pharisee, that is, he belonged to the most disciplined, the most strict sect of the Jewish religion. He gave himself to an illimitable zeal in behalf of the tradition of the fathers, opposing the "heresy" of the Christian faith. He hailed into prison men and women who were suspected of embracing the Nazarene way. When Stephen was stoned, they laid their garments at his young feet. He persecuted "this way" unto the death. And having letters from the high priest, he went to Damascus to bring back men and women bound that they might be turned over even to death or to imprisonment because they had found salvation in Jesus Christ.

It was in the midst of that zeal—that earnest, zealous commitment of his life to the faith of his fathers, to the tradition of the elders, to the Jewish religion—it was in the midst of that fervent defense of the Judaean faith that suddenly, without announcement (he did not know it but God knew it; before he was born this heavenly purpose was in the mind of the almighty God), on the way to Damascus there appeared to him above the brightness and the glory of the meridian sun the form, the face, the figure of the Son of God. Struck down in blindness by the glory of that light, he fell at the feet of the risen and glorified Lord and said, "Who art thou?" It was then that the Lord replied: "I am Jesus whom thou persecutest. But rise, and stand upon thy feet: for I have appeared unto thee for this purpose, to make thee a minister and a witness both of these things which thou hast seen, and of those things in the which I will appear unto thee; Delivering thee from the people, and from the Gentiles, unto whom now I send thee, to open their eyes, and to turn them from darkness to light, and from the power of Satan unto God, that they may receive forgiveness of sins, and inheritance among them which are sanctified by faith that is in me" (Acts 26:15-18). Recounting this dramatic story to King Agrippa, he added these words, "Whereupon, O king Agrippa, I was not disobedient unto the heavenly vision: But shewed first unto them of Damascus, and at Jerusalem, and throughout all the coasts of Judaea, and then to the Gentiles, [to the uttermost parts of the earth], that they should repent and turn to God, and do works meet for repentance" (Acts 26:19, 20). This is the call and the ministry from heaven placed in the hands of this Saul of Tarsus.

Witnessing to Men Everywhere

Wherever men were, there did Paul preach: on the river bank to a group of women in prayer meeting in Philippi; in the Agora, in the heart of the great intellectual city of Athens; and upon Mars Hill before the Areopagus (the Athenium Supreme Court); in ships battered and beaten by raging winds; before Felix and Festus, Roman procurators; before Agrippa, king of the Jews; and finally, before Nero and the Praetorian Guard—wherever he could, he witnessed to the grace of God in Christ Jesus.

And that is our call, our paragon, our example. Under the shade of a tree, on a city street, in a private home, anywhere is a good place to speak of what Christ has done for us. One does not need to know commentaries and one does not need to study Greek and Hebrew to comment and expatiate on 1 Timothy 1:15, "This is a faithful saying . . . Christ Jesus came into the world to save sinners; of whom I am chief." The carpenter can lay down his saw and his hammer and say that to a workman by his side. A blacksmith can take off his apron and lay down his iron tongs and say that to a man who happens to be in the shop. A secretary can prayerfully witness to someone as she works in an office in one of those tall buildings. To someone seated by your side, there can be some good words said about Jesus and what He has done for you. "And his grace which was bestowed upon me was not in vain; but I laboured more abundantly than they all" (1 Cor. 15:10). It is a high prerogative and a holy assignment, it is an open door and an infinite privilege for the child of God to speak a good word for Jesus. Do it.

Chapter 4

JUSTIFICATION BY FAITH

> Knowing that a man is not justified by the works of the law, but by the faith of Jesus Christ, even we have believed in Jesus Christ, that we might be justified by the faith of Christ, and not by the works of the law: for by the works of the law shall no flesh be justified.
>
> For I through the law am dead to the law, that I might live unto God.
>
> I do not frustrate the grace of God: for if righteousness come by the law, then Christ is dead in vain.
>
> (Gal. 2:16, 19, 21)

If there is any key to the gospel preached by the Apostle Paul, it is that we are saved by grace and not by works. He wrote that gospel in this letter to the churches of Galatia, the churches that he founded on his first missionary journey. He wrote it in a white heat. The very composition of the book is a thunderbolt. He wrote the same treatise, the same gospel message, in his letter to the church at Rome. The difference between these letters is that in the letter to the churches of Galatia he is a fury. The message is a fire in his bones. He has been greatly disturbed. On the other hand, the letter he wrote to Rome concerning the same subject is deliberately studied. It is like a theological treatise. But both letters are alike in their gospel content.

The Jerusalem Confrontation

Galatians 2:1 reads like this, "Then fourteen years after I went up again to Jerusalem with Barnabas, and took Titus [who had been converted directly out of his idolatry and paganism to the Christian faith] with me also." "Fourteen years later," that is, fourteen years after the days following the conversion of the apostle described in the first chapter of Galatians. At that time Paul went up to Jerusalem and there faced the Judaizers. These heretics said that a man cannot be converted and saved just by trusting the Lord, but he had also to keep certain rites, rituals, ceremonies, and to be obedient to the Mosaic law. Now the gospel of Paul states that a man can be saved just by trusting the Lord. Nothing else need be added. Not trusting Christ *and* keeping a ritual, not believing in the Lord *and* obeying certain precepts and commandments. Paul preached that a man can be saved out of idolatry, out of heathenism, out of paganism just by trusting Christ, looking to Him for forgiveness and salvation. Well, so violently opposed to such a gospel were some of those who felt that one also had to keep laws and commandments, precepts, and rituals, that the church called a conference of its leaders in Jerusalem. That conference is described in Acts 15. This happened after Paul's first missionary journey. It happened after the founding of the churches in Galatia. So when he says, "fourteen years after I went up to Jerusalem," he is referring to Acts 15. Barnabas, who was also a Hellenistic convert to Christ, accompanied him, as did Titus, a heathen, pagan Greek who had been saved just by looking to Jesus.

In that doctrinal confrontation in Jerusalem, the apostle says, "And that because of false brethren unawares brought in, who came in privily to spy out our liberty which we have in Christ Jesus, that they might bring us into bondage [under the yoke of all of those ceremonies and rites and laws]: To whom we gave place by subjection, no, not for an hour" (Gal. 2:4, 5a). He never withdrew an inch, not a millimeter. Then in the ninth verse he says, "And when James [the Lord's brother, the pastor of the church at Jerusalem], Cephas [that is, Simon Peter] and John [the beloved disciple], who seemed to be pillars, perceived the grace that was given unto me, they gave to me and Barnabas the right hands of fellowship; that we should go unto the heathen [Gentiles], and they unto the circumcision [Jews]" They divided the ministry of the church right there.

When people lament over denominations, I think they are wasting their energies. If denominations were so vile, the Spirit of God might be trying to war against them. But I do not sense any disposition on the part of the Spirit of God to uproot denominational persuasions. Here in the beginning the apostles decided that they were going to have two denominations. One would be Hebrew. It would be Jewish. The Christians in that church were to keep the law to their hearts' content—worship in the Temple, circumcise their children, and observe the feasts of the Jews. Worshiping like Jews and yet being Christians, they would have James, the Lord's brother, as their pastor. They would have Simon Peter as their great exponent and John the beloved disciple as one of their fellow workers and compeers. But it was also decided that Barnabas and Saul of Tarsus (later called Paul) should go to the heathen. While these other disciples worked with the Jews, they, Barnabas, Paul, Silas, and the rest of them, would work with the Gentiles. I see no wrong if Episcopalians love a quiet, beautiful ritual (and it is beautiful), by which they serve God, and I stand here in this pulpit and thunder so loud that people's ears hurt. When you hear people lamenting over denominations as though they were an unimpeachable evil, forget it. It is going to be that way as long as men are free to express themselves. There are some people who like to hear one sing from Handel's *Messiah*, and there are some people who like to sing pentecostal songs and clap their hands and tap their feet. I think both are all right. Maybe we can win more people to God, worshiping Him in such different ways.

The Confrontation in Antioch

"But when Peter was come to Antioch, I withstood him to the face, because he was to be blamed" (Gal. 2:11). When Peter was visiting in Antioch where the people were Gentile Chritsians, he lived and acted and ate and washed his hands (or did not wash his hands) according to Gentile custom. But when the brethren from James came from Jerusalem, Simon Peter dissembled and went back to those Jewish practices that pleased the Judaizers. He even sided with the ceremonial party which sought to make these Gentiles keep those same ordinances. Against such hypocrisy of the doctrine, Paul bitterly inveighs. This leads him to write in the following verses of justification by faith, "Knowing that a man is not justified by the works of the law, but by the faith of Jesus Christ, even we have believed in Jesus Christ, that we might be justified by the faith of Christ, and not by the works of the law: for by the works of the law shall no flesh be justified. I do not frustrate the grace of God; for if righteousness come by the law, then Christ is dead in vain." (Gal. 2:16, 21). If I could further define the preaching ministry of Paul (the Gospel that he preached) in a sentence, I would choose it in Ephesians 2:8, 9, "For by grace are ye saved through faith; and that not of yourselves: it is the gift of God: Not of works, lest any man should boast."

Oh, the reaction of Paul against Judaizers was vigorous and polemical in defense of the Gospel that he said he received by revelation from Jesus Christ in heaven. He gave place "no, not for an hour," he said, to those who would seek to bring the Gentile Christians under the bondage of the yoke of ceremonial law. Christians are free, and the defense of that liberty in Christ is this letter to the churches in Galatia. As the apostle speaks, he seeks to keep even the thin edge of a wedge of salvation by works from being insinuated into the churches.

I cannot help as I read these verses but be impressed with the outspoken courage of the apostle as he speaks of his gospel that he received from Christ Himself. One does not find in him "any faith or religion is just as good as another." You do not find in him any "one could be a Mohammedan, one could be a Buddhist, one could be a Shintoist, or one could be a Zoroastrian just as well as he could be a Christian." There is not in him any lukewarm, half-way, half-convinced commitment. He is all out and is bold to proclaim it.

It is difficult to believe that Simon Peter would cower before the ceremonialists from Jerusalem. It is even more difficult to believe that Barnabas could be carried away by this dissimulation (Gal. 2:13). Why, Simon Peter was the chief of the apostles, and Baranabas was the first Spirit-filled leader of the Christians at Antioch. How is it that Paul is able to confront them and to denounce them to their faces? Where did Paul get that authority? Did he have certificates and letters from a hierarchy, from a church, from a synod, from a convention, or from a presbytery? No! That courage came from the conviction of truth in the revelation of Jesus Christ Himself.

I do not know of a real emissary from heaven, a prophet of God, but who has that same fearless, bold, uncompromising spirit. Do you remember the story of Amos? He was an ignorant farmer, a herdsman, and a gatherer of sycamore fruit. He pinched the little buds in the sycamore trees in order that they might be more prolific in bearing fruit. And the Lord God sent him up to Bethel to preach where Jeroboam had built those golden calves. Amos stood there and denounced the idolatry of the land and the heathenism of the Israelite king, Jeroboam II. When Amaziah, the prelate of the king, the high priest of the chapel, heard Amos, he went to Jeroboam and said that the man must be hushed, for the land could not bear his word. Amaziah said to the king, "You shut him up." But Jeroboam II said: "You shut him up. You try it." So Amaziah stood before Amos the prophet of God and said to him: "You ignoramus. You herdsman, you sheep-keeper, you farmer, you sycamore pincher. You go back down to Tekoa, and there you preach and prophesy; but not here, for this is the king's chapel and the king's court." It was then that Amos said those famous words: "It is true that I am no prophet, neither am I a prophet's son; it is true that I am a herdsman, and a gatherer of sycamore fruit: And the Lord took me as I followed the flock, and the Lord said to me, Go, prophesy to my people Israel" (cf. Amos 7:14, 15). And then his thundering sentence, "The lion hath roared, who will not fear? the Lord God hath spoken, who can but prophesy?" (Amos 3:8).

That is the spirit of the prophet of God which is found also in Athanasius as he stood before the papal legate, in Martin Luther as he stood before the Diet of Worms, in John Knox as he stood before Mary, Queen of Scots, in Obadiah Holmes, a faithful Baptist deacon and preacher, as he stood before Governor Winthrop of Massachusetts when they beat him until the blood ran into his shoes. This is always the spirit of the messenger from heaven—bold, courageous, unafraid, and fearless. Thus the Apostle Paul stands and condemns Simon Peter to his face. Thus he boldly writes to the churches of Galatia. Against the subtle doctrine of salvation by self-righteousness, Paul emphasizes "that a man is not justified by the works of the law, but by the faith of Jesus Christ." He further plainly states that "by the works of the law shall no flesh be justified." Then he adds, "I do not frustrate the grace of God: for if righteousness come by the law, then Christ is dead in vain" (Gal. 2:16, 21).

Why the Doctrine of Justification by Works Is So Persistent

Why is it that the gospel of justification by works (that is, salvation by self-merit, salvation by self-righteousness) has been so persistent a doctrine through the ages? However one tries to destroy it or war against it, it is hydra-headed. It rises up again and again. Why is that? One reason is that it is personally attractive. It has an appeal to it. It ministers to our pride. We all are afflicted with a weakness that never departs, that never fails to be present in our fallen humanity, and that weakness is that we like to think well of ourselves. Our persuasion that our goodnesses and our righteousnesses and our self-merit save us ministers to our pride and to our egotism. Persistent through the years is the conviction on the part of people that, "If I do so-and-so I will merit thus-and-so." They say to themselves, "If I observe this ritual, if I obey this commandment, if I make this sacrifice, if I suffer this hurt, if I give up this practice, if I mortify my body or afflict my flesh or persecute my soul, then in that flagellation and mortification I will commend myself to God."

An extreme instance of self-persecution in order to seek praises from God appeared in an article from the United Press. "A mother of seven children burned herself at the stake in the hope of becoming a saint, police reported Wednesday. Officrs said that Angelida Borsen, 48, piled up straw and soaked it and herself with gasoline. Then she tied and gagged herself and set fire to the straw. I shall die, she said in a note, like Joan of Arc and my soul will be received in the kingdom of heaven. Mrs. Borsen, afflicted with cancer, got up every night in her farm home to pray. She read the Bible constantly and became convinced that her illness stemmed from her sins, her family said. Relatives said apparently she hoped that by dying in a terrible fashion her sins would be atoned." How tragic! But the doctrine of justification by self-righteousness, by self-merit, is of the flesh and ministers to human pride. "If I do these things, if I suffer these things, if I obey these things, then I will commend myself to God and I can be saved. *I* can do it."

Not only is self-justification a persistent and appealing doctrine to our fallen human nature, but it sounds plausible. One can almost say that it is a self-evident truth. And if you are an empiricist, you could say it has great practical value. You could point out that people must be taught and trained to be good and to be righteous and to keep all of those commandments that are pleasing to God. The doctrine seems to vindicate itself on account of its practical value. We ought to preach salvation by good works because the method would encourage virtue.

There is, however, a strange thing in the response of human behavior to this doctrine. History proves just the opposite from what one would expect. Where do you find a truly devout, upright, godly man who glories in his works? Only by faith in Jesus, only by looking to Him, is the Christian inspired to holiness and purity. Preaching good works to a fallen humanity but emphasizes the weakness of human flesh.

This doctrine of self-merit is the common denominator of all false religions. However religions may differ in a thousand categories, they all have this one feature in common: that we save ourselves by doing good, by keeping commandments, by observing rituals, by doing things—the work that supposedly commends us to God.

The Superfluity of Grace and Mercy in Self-Righteousness

Why does Paul say that self-righteousness is a denial of the Gospel of the Son of God? There are three reasons: first, if we believe that we can save ourselves, that we are meritorious, virtuous, and self-commendable in ourselves, then there is no need for the grace and the mercy of God.

An illustration of the superfluity of grace and mercy in self-righteousness is found in the instance of a man who stands before the bar of a federal court. He is innocent of that of which he has been accused. So he stands before the judge and says, "I am innocent; I am not guilty." But the judge replies, "I know that, and this court will show you mercy and grace." The man rightly and indignantly replies: "Mercy? Judge, your honor, what do you mean by mercy? I do not want mercy! I am innocent. I am not guilty, and all that I ask of this court is justice. I want my rights, because I am not a culprit or a criminal. I am innocent! And I do not want mercy!" If a man pleads mercy from a judge, that means he is guilty, he has done wrong. And he casts himself upon the mercy of the court. He cries: "May the court be merciful, may the court be forgiving, may the court be thoughtful, may the court be sympathetic, may the court be understanding. I cast myself upon the sympathies of the court and I ask for mercy." That is if the man had done wrong.

Now it is the same thing in our standing in the presence of God. If a man can stand in the presence of God and say: "Lord, I am innocent, I have never sinned. There has never been evil in my heart. There has never been wrong in my life. I am no transgressor. I have obeyed perfectly all that God has recorded of me from the day I was born, and I stand here in this court asking for justice. That is all. Just give me my rights." Then the Lord God can say: "How excellent! There has never been evil in your heart and life. Walk, perfect you, into the presence of my kingdom. Welcome, perfect you." That is like the Pharisee who stood by himself and said: "Lord, I thank Thee that I am not like other men. Why, I fast twice a week, I keep all of the commandments, and I am perfect in all my ways." When he went to bed at night, he congratulated himself on having obtained such marvelous virtue and purity. When he got up the next morning, he rubbed his hands together and congratulated himself in pride and self-righteousness. That is the doctrine of justification by works, by self-merit. But when a man stands in the presence of the mighty God, what does he say before Him? In His presence the very heavens are not pure, and He charges the angels themselves with folly. What do we say? We have to admit that we are all alike. We bow our heads and say, "Lord, I confess to Thee that I am a lost, dying person."

In one of my pastorates there was a young fellow, gifted

and brilliant, who was accused of embezzling from the bank. He was a smart boy and he thought that by juggling those books he could take money out of the bank undiscovered. He took thousands of dollars. But one is never *that* smart. They found him and accused him. When he was tried before the federal judge, the mother and the father of the boy asked me to stand by him. So we went to the big city and that boy stood before the bar and the judge seated behind the bar looked at him and asked a simple question, "Guilty or not guilty?" And the boy replied humbly and simply, "Guilty." I was standing there by his side. And you know that I had the feeling then that I represented all humanity when I stood by that lad and the judge asked, "Guilty or not guilty?" If you are not guilty and can save yourself, then the grace and mercy of God is superfluous. There is no need of the Savior. But if you are a sinner, and if you are a dying man, all of us alike are like that lad who looked back into the face of the judge and said, "Sir, your honor, I cast myself upon the mercy of the court." In that instance, the judge was so merciful to the young bank employee that he gave him a sentence and then probated it. I helped him live out that probation through the years that followed. It is thus with us. As sinners we cast ourselves upon the grace and mercy of God.

Justification by Works Makes Unnecessary the Atonement of Christ

Second, the gospel of justification by works (that we can save ourselves by what we are able to do) makes superfluous, unnecessary, ("in vain" Paul says in Gal. 2:21) the atonement of Christ. One does not need it. Look at the words that Paul uses here in Galatians 2:21, "I do not *frustrate* the grace of God." The word translated "frustrate" is *abeto,* which means "to nullify," "to regard as useless." If righteousness comes by the law, then Christ is dead "in vain." The word translated "in vain" is *dorean,* which is an adverb meaning "without cause," "groundless," translated here "in vain." If a man can save himself in self-righteousness and self-merit, there is no need for the death of Christ. He died as Paul writes it, *dorean*—"in vain," needlessly, groundlessly. There is no need for the new covenant. Let us just keep the old covenant—do good works and live. There is no need for the suffering of Christ. There is no need for Calvary. There is no need for blood atonement. There is no need for the cross—we can save ourselves.

The Praises of Heaven Are Directed not Toward Ourselves but Toward Our Savior

Third, not only does the gospel of justification by works, by self-merit (that we can save ourselves) negate the grace and mercy of God, and not only does it negate the necessity for the cross of Christ, but third, it hushes all of the hallelujahs that you will read in the Book of Revelation. What do they sing in glory? What are those praises and hallelujahs in glory? Without exception they are directed toward Christ and toward Him alone. Look in the first chapter of the Apocalypse, "Unto him that loved us, and washed us from our sins in his own blood, ... to him be glory and dominion for ever and ever" (Rev. 1:5, 6b). Or, as in the fifth chapter of the Apocalypse, "Worthy is the Lamb that was slain to receive power, and riches, and wisdom, and strength, and honour, and glory, and blessing" (Rev. 5:12). "For thou ... hast redeemed us to God by thy blood out of every kindred, any tongue, and people, and nation; And hast made us unto our God kings and priests: and we shall reign on the earth" (Rev. 5:9b, 10). Hallelujah! Amen! That is the praise of heaven.

You will not find in the Book nor will you find in glory anyone standing with the redeemed and saying: "Unto *me* be the glory. *I* did it. Unto *me* be praise and glory. *I* kept the commandments. *I* observed the ceremonies and the rituals. *I* never transgressed. *I* never fell. *I* never sinned. *I* am here because *I* did it." The whole spirit of heaven is in some other world. It is always unto *Him.* For I was lost and undone and dying, and He lifted me out of the miry clay, from the depths of the horrible pit and placed my feet on the rock. His blood washed me clean and white. "These are they who have washed their robes and made them white in the blood of the Lamb. Unto him be glory and honor and dominion forever and ever. For He has saved us by His blood, out of every nation, tribe, and family under the sun." That is the spirit of the true servant of Christ always. Job at one time vindicated his own righteousness and volitively spoke of his own good deeds. He did that in Job 41. But when he came to chapter 42, he said: "Lord, in days past I just heard about you. Now I see you and I abhor myself and I repent in dust and ashes." That is the spirit of the true child and disciple and servant of God. He humbly avows, "Lord, it is not my work, it is Christ's worthiness." It is not my strength, it is His, loving us when we are unlovely. Our Savior is always compassionate and sympathetic toward us when we come before Him with a humble petition, "Lord, remember me." He saves us, He forgives us. That is why Jesus came, thus to extend to us heaven's grace and forgiveness. That is the Gospel of Paul, it is the Gospel of Christ, it is the Gospel of that blessed Book, and it is our hope now and in the eternity to come.

Chapter 5

DIFFERING DENOMINATIONS

> And when James, Cephas, and John, who seemed to be pillars, perceived the grace that was given unto me, they gave to me and Barnabas the right hands of fellowship; that we should go unto the heathen, and they unto the circumcision. (Gal. 2:9)

In Galatians 2 Paul writes, "Then fourteen years after I went up again to Jerusalem with Barnabas, and took Titus with me also. And I went up by revelation, and I communicated unto them that gospel which I preach among the Gentiles, but privately to them which were of reputation, lest by any means I should run, or had run, in vain. But neither Titus, who was with me, being a Greek, was compelled to be circumcised: And that because of false brethren unawares brought in, who came in privily to spy out our liberty which we have in Christ Jesus, that they might bring us into bondage: To whom we gave place by subjection, no, not for an hour; that the truth of the gospel might continue with you.... And when James [the pastor of the church at Jerusalem], Cephas [Simon Peter], and John [the beloved disciple], who seemed to be pillars, perceived the grace that was given unto me, they gave to me and Barnabas the right hands of fellowship; that we should go unto the heathen, and they unto the circumcision" (vv. 1-5, 9).

Free Men Will Always Differ

There is an unfailing characteristic of humanity and it is this: if men are free, they will differ. The only way to make everyone alike is by coercion. Free men are never alike of themselves. That is true in the political world. Men differ politically and we have differing political parties, philosophies of government, approaches, outreaches, solutions. Men differ. That is true in the academic world. There are numerous theories and hypotheses that are fought or favored in the university world. That is true in the cultural and artistic worlds. There are all kinds of tastes. In music and in art, men differ. That is true in every area of life and it is certainly true in the religious world. For example, there are many different kinds of Islamic faiths. When one thinks of Buddhism, he thinks of one religion, but there are many separated sects in the Buddhist faith. When one thinks of Hinduism, he thinks of one religion, but there are many separating, differing kinds of Hinduism. When one thinks of Judaism, he thinks of one faith but there are at least three different expressions of Judaism found in the orthodox synagogue, in the conservative synagogue, and in the reform synagogue. And that characterization, that phenomenon, that tendency to differ certainly is found in the Chritsian history.

Differing groups have characterized the Christian faith from the beginning. Here in Galatians 2 we read Paul's personal account of the vigorous confrontation between him and the Judaizing Christians who sought to make all who accepted Christ also accept the Mosaic legislation. And it is specifically recorded that the differing parties agreed to divide. Some of them would go to the Jews and preach the Gospel of Christ, allowing them to keep the Jewish ceremonial laws. But there were others such as Paul who took the message to the Gentiles, separate and apart from the Mosaic legislation.

Differing interests and interpretations of men, causing divisions and denominations, characterized the Christian faith with increasing and emphatic proliferation from the beginning. There were the Ebionites, the Jewish sect which was one of the first denominations. Another early developing sect was the Marcionites, liberally orientated. There were the ascetic Montanists. There were the Dontanists, the Paulicians, the Waldensians, the Arians, the Nestorians, the Eutychians, the Monophysites, the Sabellians, the Roman Catholic Latin Church, and the Greek Catholic Eastern Church. Through the years there has been that characterization of the Christian faith, its breaking up into denominational, sectarian groups.

Sometimes the denominations are named after their form of government. The Episcopalians were named from the Greek word *episcopos,* meaning "overseer," translated in the King James Version, "bishop." The Episcopalian Church was named from its form of government, a church ruled by bishops. The Presbyterian Church received its name from the Greek word *presbuteros* meaning "elder," a church that is governed by "elders," by synods and sessions and presbytries. The Congregational Church is a church that is governed by its own congregation. These are denominations that are named for their form of government.

Sometimes the denomination will be named for the man who founded it, such as the Lutheran Church, and the Mennonite Church. Sometimes the church will be named from the place of its origin, such as the Moravian Church from Moravia. Sometimes the church has a self-chosen name such as the Catholic Church, the Nazarene Church, the Church of God, or the Church of Christ. Sometimes the church is nicknamed, such as the Christians were nicknamed Chritsians, *Christionoi,* in Antioch. The Mormon church, whose actual name is the Church of the Latter-day Saints, is nickamed from Mormon. The Baptist church is a nickname. They were first called Anabaptists because when people who said they were baptized as infants, became converts to this faith, they were baptized again. *Ana,* the Greek word "again," so Anabaptist represented rebaptized people. Later the first syllable was omitted and they were called "Baptists." Thus we find the proliferation of denominations through all of the centuries from the bargaining here in the Scriptures to this present hour.

Now denominations differ over anything and everything and new denominations rise again and again. There is no part of the work in which one will not find that differentiation and finally the breaking up into denominational groups. For example, in about 1830 to 1840 there was a big schism, a division in our Baptist churches over baptism. There was a brilliant, able, capable minister and expositor of the Scriptures by the name of Alexander Campbell. He began to preach that we have to be baptized in order to be saved. To us the Scriptures say explicitly that the blood of Christ cleanses us from all sin: "and the blood of Jesus Christ his Son cleanseth us from all sin" (1 John 1:7). But he began to preach that the water baptism cleansed our sin. We are washed from our sins in water baptism. The doctrine created a violent division in the church, and the churches divided. Out of that division came the Campbellite movement, which itself split into two parts—the Disciples of Christ, or the Christian Church, and the Church of Christ, the conservative wing of it. These denominations came about over a schism concerning baptism or the purpose of baptism.

Men have divided again and again in the story of Christendom over the Lord's Supper. When the great Reformation started under Martin Luther, there was another great reformer who lived in Zurich, Switzerland, by the name of Zwingli. It was thought that the entire Reform Movement could be brought together if Martin Luther and Zwingli could share in a personal discussion, could talk to one another face to face. Their agreement would bring together the entire movement. So Martin Luther met with Zwingli. They agreed on doctrinal point after doctrinal point in an effort to join the forces of the Reformation together. But when they came to the Lord's Supper, there was no solution for them. Martin Luther was a monk in the Catholic Church, and all of his life he had been taught the doctrine of transubstantiation; that is, the power of the priest to convert the bread and the wine into the actual body and blood of Jesus. When Martin Luther came out of the Catholic church, he brought with him a part of those doctrinal persuasions. Martin Luther's idea of the Lord's Supper is called consubstantiation, that is, the elements are not actually, miraculously transformed into the body and blood of Christ but they coexist with the body and blood of Christ in an unusual and miraculous way—consubstantiation. Well, Zwingli believed that the elements of the Lord's Supper were nothing but symbols of the body and blood of Christ and that the ordinance was a symbolic ordinance held in remembrance of Christ; that is, their purpose is to bring back to our memory the passion, the suffering, the sacrifice, the cross, the blood of Christ. When those men began to discuss the Lord's Supper they violently differed over it. Martin Luther said to Zwingli that the Scriptures plainly depict the Lord as saying, "This is My body and this is My blood." But Zwingli said the word *is*, the verb "to be," means "represents." Martin Luther said the Bible does not say, "This bread represents My body, this cup represents My blood," rather, the Scriptures say, "This *is* my body, this *is* my blood." Zwingli said, "But the word 'is' means 'represents'." Luther thundered, 'Where does it say in the Bible or where is it used in the Bible, that the verb 'to be,' 'is' means 'represents'?" Zwingli replied that in the forty-first chapter of the Book of Genesis in Joseph's interpretation of the dream that Pharaoh had of the seven lean cows that ate up the seven good cows, and the seven bad ears of corn that ate up the seven good ears, there the Scriptures state that the seven good cows *are* seven years of plenty, and the seven ill-looking cows *are* the seven years of draught, and the seven good ears of corn *are* the seven years of plenty and the seven bad ears of corn *are* the seven years of famine. Zwingli thus avowed that the verb "to be" can mean "pictures," "represents." But the men in violent disagreement separated, Martin Luther continued with the Lutheran Church. Zwingli and the Evangelical Church of Switzerland continued—two denominations supporting their violent difference over the meaning of the Lord's Supper.

One time I spoke at a conference in California in which there were eleven different kinds of Baptists. I preached one time in the mountains of eastern Kentucky, and I found there were twelve different denominations of Baptists in that one county. One denomination was "Spittin' Baptists," and another denomination was "Two Seeds in the Spirit Predestinarian Baptists. Dividing over anything, over everything—this has characterized the Christian faith from the beginning.

Our Attitude Toward Other Denominations

Now what shall be our attitude toward the denomination? First, our attitude ought always to be one of respect for the other man's opinion and interpretation. He does not see it as I do, he does not preach it the way I try to preach it, he does not understand it as I understand it, he does not interpret it as I interpret it, but I first of all ought to look upon him and his opinion with love and charity. I can easily imagine a three-way argument between Bartimaeus, the blind man whom Jesus healed in Mark 10, and another blind man whom Jesus healed in John 9, and yet another blind man whom Jesus healed in Matthew 20. They are in a violent argument over how Jesus opens the eyes of the blind. Bartimaeus says: "I know exactly how Jesus opens the eyes of the blind. He speaks the word and it is done. I know that because I was blind and that is the way He healed me." And the second blind man (whose story is found in the twentieth chapter of the Book of Matthew) says: "That is not so. I know exactly how Jesus opens the eyes of the blind. He takes His hand and He touches the eyes, and the eyes are opend. I know bcause that is the way He opened my eyes." And the blind man who was healed in John 9 says: "Both of you are certainly and absolutely wrong. I know exactly how Jesus opens the eyes of the blind. He spits on the ground and makes clay of the spittle and anoints the eyes of the blind and tells them to go to the pool of Siloam and wash and their eyesight returns. I know because I was blind and that is the way He opened my eyes." The bitter argument goes around and around and around. Well, the truth of the matter is that all of them were right.

There is a famous poem written by the famous American editor, humorist, and lecturer about the six blind men of Indostan, the blind men and the elephant, which concerns theological arguments. Do you remember it?

> It was six men of Indostan
> To learning much inclined,
> Who went to see the elephant
> 'Though all of them were blind.
> That each by observation
> Might satisfy his mind.
>
> The first approached the elephant
> And happening to fall against
> His broad and sturdy side,
> At once began to bawl,
> "God bless me but the elephant
> Is just like a wall."
>
> The second, feeling of the tusk

Cried, "Ho, what have we here.
So very round and smooth and sharp
To me 'tis mighty clear
This wonder of an elephant
Is very like a spear."

The third approached the animal
And happening to take
A squirming trunk within his hand
Thus boldly up and spake,
"I think that he the elephant
Is very like a snake."

The fourth reached out an eager hand
And felt about the knee;
"What most this wondrous beast is like
Is mighty plain," quote he,
"Tis clear enough the elephant
Is very like a tree."

The fifth who came to touch the ear
Said, "E'en the blindest man
Can tell what this resembles most,
Deny the fact who can.
This marvel of an elephant
Is very like a fan."

The sixth no sooner had begun
About the beast to grope,
Than, seizing on the swinging tail,
That fell within his scope;
"I say," quote he, "The elephant
Is very like a rope."

And so these men of Indostan
Disputed loud and long,
Each in his opinion
Exceeding stiff and strong.
Though each was partly in the right,
And all were in the wrong.

And now, the closing stanza reveals the moral as to why the author wrote the poem:

So oft, in theologic wars
The disputants, I ween,
Rail on in utterance of
What each other mean,
And prate about an elephant
Not one of them has seen."

—John Godfrey Saxe (1816-1887)

We may not, in the Christian faith, ever come to see alike

or ever come to think alike, but in the Christian faith, always there ought to be reverence for one another's understanding and peace and love in our hearts for the Christian Community.

Our Faithful Attitude Toward What We Believe

Now the second attitude that I think ought to characterize us is that we ought to be true to what we believe. I may not believe as that man believes, but I ought to be sincere, and true and faithful in what I do believe, and preach the truth as under God, humbly, prayerfully, I understand it and see it. This sense of loyalty to my understanding of the Scriptures makes me a denominationalist. For example, I would have great difficulty, having read the Bible and studied it, in baptizing an infant. Years ago I went to Brown University and then to Yale University for my theological education. As a youth, having been graduated from Baylor, I was invited to pastor a little church in Rhode Island. They said they would pay my expenses while I pursued my Master of Arts degree in Brown and then my Doctor of Philosophy degree in Yale. When I discussed with the men of the church about my accepting the pastorate, I asked them about the administration of the ordinances, and they said: "You do not have to burden your heart about that. We do not observe any ordinances in this church. We do not baptize and we do not have the Lord's Supper. So you will not be embarrassed." "Well," I thought, "that is marvelous. I won't be embarrassed. The incident of a mother coming up to me, bringing her baby and asking me to baptize the infant, will not occur." But it weighed on my heart that I would be pastor of a church that did not observe the ordinances. So I finally turned aside into another channel and into another direction. I would have trouble baptizing an infant, but I can't help that.

In another area I would have great difficulty. If a man came to me and said: "I am the bishop and we are going to take you out of the First Baptist Church in Dallas. You have been here twenty-eight years and that is long enough for anybody. We are going to take you out of the First Baptist Church in Dallas and we are going to put you over here in the First Baptist Church of some town unknown to me—well, I would have difficulty in this because I feel that the Spirit of

God led me (and the people were led of the Spirit of God who called me) to this pastorate. This is God's place for me. And now a man who says he is a bishop is proposing to take me and put me some other place, assign me to another congregation. I would have difficulty in that.

A third difficulty for me would be if somebody came to me and said: "You've got to stand in that pulpit and preach that we are saved again and again and again. You can be saved and you can be lost. And whether you get to heaven or not depends upon just what little piece of your life you happen to die in, because if you die in that lost piece, man, you're going to hell, but if you die in that saved piece you're going to heaven. So you have to be very careful in what little piece of your life you die in, because you can be saved and lost." I would have difficulty with that doctrine! Jesus said: "I give unto them eternal life and they shall never perish, neither shall anyone pluck them out of My hand. My Father who gave them to Me is greater than all and no one is able to pluck them out of My Father's hand" (cf. John 10:23, 29). "He that believeth hath eternal life." Well, how long is that? Until tomorrow or until next month or until five years from now? Just how long is "eternal"? I would have difficulty preaching the doctrine that one can be saved and lost because my own experience has been that if people are ever genuinely saved, they never get away from it. They may backslide, and they may fall into all kinds of difficulty and aberration, but they never get away from it. The seed of God, as John says in the first epistle, stays in his heart. One sure sign of regeneration is that if one has ever been born again, he will never get away from it. I would have difficulty preaching the doctrine that one can be saved and lost, as though Christ died for us over and over again. Each time we were saved He would have to die for us again. It is as though His sacrifice on the cross was not sufficient. I would have difficulty with that doctrine. So the best thing for me to do is just to admit and confess that I am a Baptist. As such, it is better for me to stay here in this church and to preach this Gospel as I read, see, and believe it and as God makes it meaningful to me. So I am happy to be a denominationalist. Dr. Truett said a sentence that stayed in my mind. I heard him say at a great convention, "I am not a sectarian, but I am a denominationalist." I feel that way. I do not want to be a sectarian in my spirit. I do not want to be divisive in my attitude. I ask God to help me to be charitable, sympathetic, understanding and kind, but under God at the same time, I ought to believe what God reveals to me, and preach it in all humility and prayerful zeal.

The Blessing of God Upon All Men Who Preach Christ

On the mission fields I see some of the most marvelous people in the world who are not Baptists. In the heart of Africa, down there in the Amazon, in some of the teeming cities of Asia, I see the Wycliffe missionary, I see the Christian and Missionary Alliance missionary, I see the Brethren missionary. When I see those people, I do not look upon them with bitterness or with sectarian contempt or hatred. I thank God for them. There in the heart of the dark continent, in the sweltering Amazon jungle, or under the Arctic Circle, there are missionaries of other denominations who are preaching Jesus. In my own spirit and attitude, I thank God for them. Even under denominational envy and strife, Paul said in the first chapter of Philippians: "Some indeed preach Christ even of envy and strife; and some also of good will: The one preach Christ of contention, not sincerely, supposing to add affliction to my bonds: But the other of love, knowing that I am set for the defence of the gospel. What then? nothwithstanding, every way, whether in pretence, or in truth, Christ is preached; and I therein do rejoice, yea, and will rejoice" (Phil. 1:15-18). When a man preaches Jesus, I do not care where he is or what, I ask sincerely God's blessing upon that man. Wherever he stands, if he preaches Jesus, God bless him, and may God give power to him.

The Lord Himself said, "There is a first commandment." He said there is also a second commandment, but there is a first commandment. Now, a deduction. There are some things that are first, primary, and fundamental in the Christian faith, and to me that fundamental doctrine in the Christian faith is Jesus. It is Christ. All other things are in second place. It is Christ and Christ alone. It is Jesus and Him only, and I repeat, God bless any man anywhere who has it in his heart to preach Jesus. So, Paul writes . . . "James, Cephas, and John . . . gave to me and Barnabas the right hands of fellowship; that we should go unto the heathen, and they unto the circumcision" (Gal. 2:9). And God bless them all—Cephas, James, John, Paul, and Barnabas.

O Lord, may I have always in my heart the spirit of love and charity, preaching Jesus.

Chapter 6

CRUCIFIED WITH CHRIST

> I am crucified with Christ: nevertheless I live; yet not I, but Christ liveth in me: and the life which I now live in the flesh I live by the faith of the Son of God, who loved me, and gave himself for me. (Gal. 2:20)

The title of this chapter "Crucified With Christ," or, "Not I, but Christ." It is based upon a most familiar passage in the Bible, Galatians 2:20: "I am crucified with Christ: nevertheless I live; yet not I, but Christ liveth in me: and the life which I now live in the flesh I live by the faith of the Son of God, who loved me, and gave himself for me." Possibly most of you have memorized that text from childhood.

Sometimes in a great mountain range there will stand up high, elevated, and lofty, a marvelous peak. One time while flying along the coast of Alaska, our Southern Baptist Missionary Chron said to me, "You know, I've been flying along here for fourteen years and this is the first time I have ever seen the weather clear." It was a beautiful day and those mountain ranges were breath taking. As we flew along there came into view a peak towering above all the others, Mount Fairweather, rising fourteen thousand feet out of the blue ocean. Solid white, it looked like a gigantic snow cone. There are texts in the Bible like that. In the great range there will be a towering verse that somehow has in it the very presence and breath of God. Pure, holy, piercing the blue of the sky, it also penetrates our deepest souls. This is one, "I am crucified with Christ: nevertheless I live; yet not I, but Christ liveth in me: and the life which I now live in the flesh I live by the faith of the Son of God, who loved me, and gave himself for me." Do you notice how many personal pronouns there are? There are eight of them in that short sentence.

The Personal Character of the Christian Faith

The text brings to mind the emphatic truth that the Christian faith is personal. It is inward, it is individual. The Christian faith is the religion of the one lost sheep, and the one lost coin, and the one lost boy. God does not look at us by gobs and buckets-full and oceans-full, but God looks at us one by one. He knows our names and He knows all about us. Sometimes looking out under the chalice of the blue sky one will see an extensive nebula in the heavens which looks like just a vast conglomerate, but if he looks at it through a telescope, he will find it to be a galaxy of individual stars. When we look at the mass of mankind we are prone to lump them all together into a vast limbo of the unknown. But God looks at mankind individually, one by one. So it is in this text. The Christian faith begins with a personal experience when we are born into the kingdom and into the family of God. There is no other way that we become a part of it except to be born personally, individually into it. We cannot become Christians by the godliness of others, nor are we Christians because we were born in a Christian family, or because we are being reared and do live in a Christian nation. Someone facetiously said one might as well say that because a fellow was born in a garage he was a car, or because a rat lives in a stable he is a horse. No! However we were born in a family or in a country, if we are Christians we are so individually, being born again into the family of God.

Not only that, but our commitment to Christ entailing our consecration of life is always personal and individual. If a "we" respond to the call of Christ it is always a "you" or an "I" who do it. If it is not the "ones" of us that become the "we" of the assembly of us, the commitment does not exist. Always that consecration is personal and individual. We give our lives to Christ one by one. We commit ourselves to our Lord one by one. Nehemiah, however others thought or did, proposed in his own heart to rebuild the walls of the Holy City.

Isaiah said, "Here am *I*, Lord, send *me*." The Apostle Paul said, "Lord, what wouldst thou have *me* to do?" When Athanasius was made aware of the fact that the whole world was against him, the great theologian replied, "Then it is *I*, Athanasius, against the whole world." Our experience is individual and personal or it is nothing at all. It is what I have felt, what I have heard, what I have known, and what I experience. Not what the faith means to others, but what it means to me. Just as no one can sleep for you, no one can wake for you, no one can eat for you, just so no one can experience God for you. No one can live your life for you. You have to live it yourself. So it is before God. Our relationship with the Lord is always something I must feel, I must see, I must know. Our baptismal service is like that, a picture of personal death and resurrection. Nobody can die for you. You must die for yourself. However there may be others around you, when you leave, when you go out, you go out alone. When you are raised from the dead you are raised personally, individually. And when you stand before God, you will stand by yourself, alone.

Paul Addressing His Fellow Christians as Though They Were Dead

Notice how Paul will speak of the dead as being alive and the living as being dead. "I am crucified with Christ: yet I live." One of the strange things in the writings of the Apostle Paul is this: that he will contsantly refer and address his hearers, his readers as being dead. In Romans 6:8, for example, Paul writes, "If we be dead with Christ." Look again at Colossians 2:20, "If ye be dead with Christ." Then again, "For ye are dead, and your life is hid with Christ in God" (Col. 3:3). And yet again, "It is a faithful saying: For if we be dead with him, we shall also live with him" (2 Tim. 2:11). Is that not strange, addressing letters and speaking to his fellow Christians as being dead! "For ye are dead in Christ." What Paul means is that the cross has cut us off from the world. We have become separate and apart from it. But we have not fallen into corruption and in decay. In the death of Christ, we are also introduced to a new and marvelous life. The terrible nails and the iron spear that separated us from the old life and the old world also opened a fountain of new life for us in God. The old man died that the new man might live. The outward man died that the inward man might come to birth. It is a shutting out of the world that we might be introduced to the light of the knowledge of the glory and life of God in Christ Jesus.

Once a year the high priest entered the Holy of Holies. When he did so, he entered a cubicle that was absolutely dark. There was no ray of the light of the world that penetrated it. When the high priest entered the Holy of Holies he shut out the world—all of it! But as he left the light of the sun and the light of the world, he was introduced to the Shekinah glory of God, the light that burned above the mercy seat. He saw it only by shutting out the light of the world. The spiritual is the opposite of the physical. Faith is the opposite of sight. The love of God is the opposite of the love of the world. If we would truly know God and see God, we must shut out the world. That is why in prayer we close our eyes that we might open the eyes of our soul, by faith, toward God.

The Meaning of the Crucified Life

"I am crucified with Christ." What does that mean? Three times in the Gospel does the Savior say, "Take up your cross and follow me." Jesus uses that expression in Matthew 10 and 14 and in Luke 14. "Take up your cross and follow me." Both expressions, that of Paul and that of Jesus, refer to the same thing. The Holy Spirit has given us two phrases to describe the same experience. "I am crucified with Christ," and "Take up your cross and follow me." But what do cross-bearing and crucifixion in Christ refer to? Some identify it with a personal sorrow, saying: "I have a burden, I have a broken heart, I have a great frustration and disappointment, I have an agony, I have a great trial. This is my cross to bear." Now, I would not deny, nor would you, that Christians, as everyone else, have trials. We have heartaches, frustrations, and despairs. But the meaning of cross-bearing in the Bible does not even approach this matter of personal affliction. When the Lord says I am to "Take up thy cross," and when Paul uses another Holy Spirit expression, "I am crucified with Christ," they are talking about dying. Crucifixion means death. A cross is to *die* on. When the Lord speaks of taking up your cross, he is talking about dying. When the Lord bore His cross and made His way to a hill called Golgotha, Calvary, He came to a place to die. The cross was an instrument of execution. From the agony on that hill the sun hid its face. The Son of God cried in desolation and loneliness, "My God, why?" It was death. That is exactly what Paul means here in "I am crucified with Christ." The Christian is dead to self, to vanity, to egotism, to all of the blandishments of the world. He is dead.

Could I summon the temerity to speak to myself? How I need this word said to me. I am to die. As dead, I am to have no feelings. There are Christians who go around with feelings on their sleeves—so easily insulted, so easily hurt, so easily made to feel unwanted or uncared for. They whine, "They don't appreciate me," or "They don't recognize me," or "They are not cognizant of my gifts," and "I'm hurt." Full of feelings! The dead do not have feelings! If I am filled with ambition, vanity, and self-seeking, then I lay myself open to all of the hurt of this world. But if I am dead to it, I can not be hurt. Oh, how I need the sermon preached to me!

How do we reach the plain in Christian growth where worldly things do not matter? "I am crucified with Christ." How do I get to the place where I can say: "I have no personal ambitions at all—just loving God. You do not need to cajole me, pat me on the back, feed me all kinds of compliments and sweetness. I was not doing it for those compliments. I was doing it for God. The old selfish life died and what is left is just, 'not I, but Christ'." O Lord, how do you get there—how do you do that—where all that you do is just for Thee—nothing of self?"

Most of us start out saying, "Lord, a whole lot of self and a little of Thee." Then as we continue to grow we add, "Some of self and some of Thee." Then as we continue to grow, we say, "Just a little of self and a lot of Thee." Finally, if we are able to grow, we say, "None of self and all of Thee." "I am crucified with Christ." Dead to self. Lord, we would be new people if we could be like that. Humble before God, just as unto the Lord. "Not I, but Christ."

James A. Garfield was the twentieth President of the United States. As President of the United States, when he came to church, the people were very conscious of his presence. Especially was the pastor proud of him. He would refer to him from the pulpit as "President James A. Garfield." One day the President came to see his pastor and said: "Pastor, I know on the outside and before the world I am the President of the United States. But in the church I am just plain James A Garfield." Is it not a beautiful story of humility? What a shame that a good man like that was assassinated.

William Carey was God's modern saint who founded the eighteenth-century missionary movement that changed the whole culture and life of India. One time he was being honored by the Governor General of India. Present at the occasion was a petty government official who looked upon the Baptist missionary with contempt. At the dinner table the petty official openly said to a friend so that William Carey could hear it, "This William Carey, I understand, was a shoe maker." It was said for the ears of the missionary, so William Carey humbly replied, "Sir, I was not a shoe maker; I was a cobbler." You cannot touch a man like that! Nor can you cut a man like that because he is dead. He has died to himself. He has died to every ambition. Yet he lives gloriously. "Not I, but Christ." "I am crucified with Christ: nevertheless I live; yet not I, but Christ liveth in me: and the life which I now live in the flesh I live by the faith of the Son of God." That kind of a death is an introduction to another life, a resurrected life.

The More Glorious Life of the Christian Resurrection

It can be easily understood how those of us who are Christians dread to face a truth like that! Called upon to die, to be crucified, how fearful! Inherently, instinctively we shun such a death. But no, we ought not be filled with such dread and such foreboding. This is a death in order that we might be resurrected to another and a golden, glorious life in God. We are resurrection people. The world's sin and death have no more power upon us. We live in the resurrected power of God. That is real life.

By comparison, look at a worldling, one who says, "Life, life, oh, I must live!" So he makes his way to the red-light district. There he seeks an abounding life. Or he makes his way to the junkie and the pusher. "Life, life!" he cries. And he gets high on drugs. "Life, man, I'm living it up!" Or he makes his way to the saloon. "Life! life!" he cries. This is life? Really? Venereal disease, is that life? In epidemic proportions does it sweep the world and is now sweeping America. That is life? The drug addict with his sallow complexion, and his destroyed mind—that is life? Or the drunkard lying in his own vomit. That is life? "I am crucified with Christ; nevertheless I live." THAT IS LIFE!

The old Saul died that the Apostle Paul might be born again. The old Saul was such a different person. He was proud in the tradition of his fathers. He was proud of his zeal. He was proud of his attainment among his peers. He even said, "I persecuted the church and I wasted the people of God in good conscience." He was proud of his heritage and proud of his commitment. But when they brought him to Damascus they were leading him by the hand. The light of the glory in Christ had struck him blind. And out of the death of the old Saul, the new Paul came to birth. Is it not so with us? We die to our old selves in order to be raised to a new life in Christ.

When we look at at the death of Christ, we see not the death of just a man, another man dying for his own sins who ought to die. No! He is our representative on the cross. And when He died, He died for us, and we died in Him. Any lawyer will tell you that when a criminal is put to death, the book is closed. The state has no more accusation against him. The penalty is paid. So it is in Christ. He died for us, and our sins, our shortcomings, and our every weakness, all of them died in Christ. Every false ambition and everything that is of self died in our Lord. It is gone. And what we have now is the glory of the presence of the Lord in Christ Jesus, what Paul refers to as, "The life which I now live in the flesh." We are not talking about a maimed, mutilated life, but a full life in Christ Jesus.

The Constraining Power of the Death of Christ for Us

The new life is motivated by a new affection. We live for "him who loved me and gave himself for me." What a beautiful way to say it! "Who loved me and gave himself for me." That is what moves the Christian Godward and lifts him heavenward. It is the constraining power of a deep affection.

There was a North American Indian who stood up and said: "There came to our tribe a man and he told us about and extolled the God of the white man. We told him to leave. And there came another man and he said: 'Do not drink any more firewater. Do not get drunk, and do not steal.' We paid no attention to him. Then there came a man and he told us about a God who came down from heaven to live among us, who so loved us that He shared our life and died in our place for our sins, and who opened the doors whereby we might be saved and enter heaven. And the Indian said, 'I could never forget it.' "

Somehow I have that persuasion about all of mankind, whether they accept it or not, whether they believe it or not, whether they are saved or not, somehow they cannot forget it. The world is not the same since Jesus died in it. And this planet somehow is not like other planets because here the foot of the cross was set and Jesus was raised beneath the sky. And we who have embraced the Lord cannot forget it. This He did for me. "Who loved me and gave himself for me." It is the love of Christ that constrains us (2 Cor. 5:14). It is the goodness of God that brings us to repentance (Rom. 2:4). It is the appealing, atoning grace, mercy, sobs, tears, and blood of our Lord that brings us and binds us to God. I somehow cannot forget it.

Chapter 7

THE BEWITCHED GALATIANS

> O foolish Galatians, who hath bewitched you, that ye should not obey the truth, before whose eyes Jesus Christ hath been evidently set forth, crucified among you?
> This only would I learn of you, Received ye the Spirit by the works of the law, or by the hearing of faith?
> Are ye so foolish? having begun in the Spirit, are ye now made perfect by the flesh? (Gal. 3:1-3)

Had the writer been Latin he would have addressed the letter to the Gauls. Had he been a modern author he would have addressed the letter to the French people. But Paul, being a member of the Hellenistic Diaspora of the Jewish people, and speaking Greek, addressed the letter to the Galatians. Whether they are Gauls in France, or whether they are Gauls in Central Asia Minor, they all belong to the same family and the Greeks called them Galatians. The Romans created a province in the center of Asia Minor and called it the Roman province of Galatia. To those churches in Galatia the Apostle Paul addressed this letter.

The apostle marveled at the hospitable, gracious reception he received, both in his own person and also in the message that he delivered. Here in the fourth chapter of the letter he says: "Ye know how through infirmity of the flesh I preached the gospel unto you at the first. And my temptation which was in my flesh ye despised not, nor rejected; but received me as an angel of God, even as Christ Jesus. Where is then the blessedness ye spake of? for I bear you record, that, if it had been possible, ye would have plucked out your own eyes, and have given them to me" (Gal. 4:13-15). He was astonished at the openhearted, warmhearted reception of the Gospel message and of the messenger himself when he preached Jesus to the Galatians. But now he is no less full of amazement at how soon they are removed from the message that they had first so gladly received. In the first chapter of the letter, after the salutation, he writes, "I marvel that ye are so soon removed from him that called you into the grace of Christ unto another gospel: Which is not another. . . ." And then in this text in the third chapter, "O foolish Galatians [O senseless Galatians], who hath bewitched you?" They had turned from Calvary to Sinai, from sonship to serfdom, from liberty and freedom to bondage, from faith to works, from Christ to ceremonies. "O senseless (foolish) Galatians, who hath bewitched you?"

The Wonderful Conversion of the Heathen Galatians

The apostle recalls their wonderful conversion. "Before whose eyes Jesus Christ hath been *prographo*," translated here "evidently set forth." "Crucified among you." *Prographo* is a word that refers to the placards that were publicly displayed in a forum or in an agora, in a market place, for all of the citizens to see. Having no newspapers, public announcements were *prographo,* they were displayed in those public areas where everyone mingled. There everyone could read them. Paul uses that word with regard to the Gospel message that was delivered to the Galatians. Jesus Christ was *prographo,* publicly, openly, "evidently set forth." When Paul preached the message of Christ, the Galatians could see the Lord crucified. They, in imagination, followed the movements of the Roman soldiers, heard the ringing of the hammers as the Lord was nailed to the tree. They heard His sobs, His tears, and His cries. They felt His suffering as they watched the blood drops fall down to encrimson the ground. Seeing Him crucified, they were convicted in their hearts, they forsook their paganism and idolatry and were born again into the kingdom of Christ. They became new creatures. The old life, the old world, the old ways passed away, and all things in God became new. They were regenerated through listening to the preached Word and through opening their hearts to the Gospel of Christ. They forsook their old gods and embraced the true and living God in Christ Jesus. It was a new and a wonderful day for the Galatians.

Let me pause here to parenthesize. You have a marvelous testimony here to the Gospel that Paul preached. What was the message that he delivered? It was that Christ died for our sins, that He was buried, and that the third day He rose again, all according to the Scriptures. When Paul preached the Gospel, that is what he preached—Christ and Him crucified. That is the faith. That is the substance and the essence of Christianity. The beginning of the Christian faith, the middle, and the end of it is the Lord Jesus. When Paul preaches the Gospel that atones for our sins and saves us from death, he is preaching Christ. When the Apostle John writes of the revelation of the Father and the eternal life through Him, he is writing about Christ. When James, the pastor of the church at Jerusalem, speaks of the great lawgiver and judge, he is talking about Christ. And when the author of the epistle to the Hebrews speaks of the great High Priest in heaven, and the mediator between God and man, he is talking about Christ. The Christian faith is Christ. Take that away—take the Lord out of it—and it is nothing.

The Gospel that Paul preached was Christ and Him crucified, and the power of it, the effect of it, upon the Galatians was glorious indeed. It was miraculous. It took the whole believing multitude of them out of idolatry and paganism and set them in the glorious liberty of the Son of God. The light of heaven was on their brow. Their lips cried, "Abba, Father," and the presence and power of Christ was in their hearts. They were a new people. They arose in Christ to liberty and life, inspired by the glorious new life in Jesus. Indeed, the transformation was miraculous.

The Equally Astonishing Backsliding of the Galatian Converts

Then they changed, then they turned—to what? There came pseudo-apostles, false teachers who took their minds away from Christ and set before them rituals, rites, seasons, dates, programs, ceremonies, and laws to keep. They turned aside from the liberty that they knew in the Lord Jesus in order to yoke themselves down in bondage to rites, ceremonies, dates, calendars, and laws. And they thought that they were making progress in doing it! They were advancing in the state of religion! Paul cries, "O senseless Galatians, who hath bewitched you? having begun in the Spirit, are ye now made perfect by the flesh?" Could I turn that into modern nomenclature? Having been gloriously saved in a revival meeting, having found the Lord as our personal Savior, having found liberty and freedom in Him, and having given ourselves to rejoicing in Christ Jesus, now we are advancing to the prison cells of the studied observance of rituals, ceremonies, laws, and commandments. Paul asks: "Is this progress? Is this advancement? To turn aside from the glorious liberty that we have in Christ in order to shackle ourselves and to bind ourselves down with calendars and ritualistic observances and the tedious, wearisome keeping of all kinds of laws? Is that advancement in the faith of true religion?"

The Galatians had backslidden. They had turned aside from the Gospel. They had taken their minds off Christ, and focused them upon something else. Whenever one does that, there is a letdown in the power of the Gospel of God. There is no such thing as finding power—regenerating, converting power—in rites and rituals, no matter what they are. Power comes only from a personal encounter with Jesus Christ, from the moving, regenerating Spirit of the Lord. Religious practices that are solely defined by observances of rituals and ceremonies are drags, they are yokes, they are bondages, they are fetters, they are chains, they are manacles. For where the Spirit of Christ is, there is liberty! When we take our hearts and our minds away from Jesus, we immediately fall into a backslidden state.

This week I read about a little Indian evangelist, a former Hindu, who was known by the name Sammy. He went around with a big Bible under one arm and carried a big umbrella above his head with his other arm. Little Sammy was trotting down a road in India when he passed by a barrack where English soldiers were stationed. They were familiar with the little preacher, so as he trotted by with his big Bible and his big umbrella, one of the British soldiers called to him and said, "Say, Sammy, how is Jesus Christ this morning?" The little fellow stopped, drew himself up to his greatest height, looked reproachfully at the soldiers, and said, "I will answer you out of the Holy Book which came to us from your country." He then turned to Hebrews 13:8 and read, "Jesus Christ the same yesterday, and to-day, and for ever." And then he trotted on up the road. That night two of those British soldiers found the modest home of little Sammy, the evangelist, knocked at the door, and when the little fellow came to the door the British soldiers said: "Sammy, we are ashamed of ourselves. This morning we asked you about how Jesus Christ was, and you read to us out of the Holy Book, 'Jesus Christ the same yesterday, to-day, and for ever.'" They said: "When we were back home, we were Christians and we served the Lord. But we have fallen away. Little Sammy, we have come to apologize and ask forgiveness for what we said this morning, and want you to know that we are coming back. We are coming back into the love and service and ministry of our dear Lord." Always it is revival, always it is true Godly service when we keep our eyes upon Him, when we rejoice in Christ our Savior.

Spiritual Freedom in Keeping Our Minds Upon Christ

Oh, but we are free when we keep our hearts on Christ and our minds stayed on Him. You would be amazed at some of the things I think in my mind. Here is a good illustration of it. We have a tendency in the Baptist Church to poke our finger at these ritualistic, liturgical services of other denominations. They follow a prayer book, they go through those same things year after year. And we have a tendency to poke our finger at them. They are just rituals, they are just ceremonies, they go over them again and again. Do you know what I think? We are exactly like them. If you do not believe it, take the format of our public worship services year after year. I am not even talking about two Sundays. I am talking about fifty-two Sundays in this current year, fifty-two in the year before, and the fifty-two Sundays in the years before that. Go back and at such-and-such a time we do such-and-such a thing, and at such-and-such a time we do the next thing, then the next stated thing, then the next stated thing, and right on down. I could close my eyes if I were in Afghanistan and know exactly what the First Baptist Church in Dallas is doing at such-and-such a time spot and at such-and-such a moment, over and over and over again.

Well, how do you get away from it? To show you how I do not know how to get away from it, I have been doing the same thing in my pulpit in Dallas for twenty-eight years. I wish that there was far greater freedom and liberty and the moving of the Spirit in our services than there is, but I do not know how to achieve it. I just have never been able to arrive at it. But I hate to think that forever our worship of God is staid, that it is straight-jacketed, that it is held in some kind of a rigorous form that nobody would dare break. You know, sometimes I wish somebody would get up in the middle of the congregation and say, "Pastor, I do not understand a word you are saying—what was that?" Well, you would think I would forget my sermon. No, sir, because I do not have it memorized. I just get up here and ask God to help me preach the message I have in my heart. You will not bother me anytime, should anybody interrupt for a holy, heavenly reason. I am not suggesting that you do it out of idiocy and inanity, but if God were to intervene in our ritual, I think it would be marvelous. If the Holy Spirit were to move in a different direction in the services and were to change the format, I would rejoice. I would thank God.

"O foolish Galatians, who hath bewitched you?" The Greek word *baskaino,* would mean that a sorcerer has placed them under a spell. *Baskaino,* "bewitched you." Paul avows that an evil eye has possessed the Galatian churches and has pulled them away from the truth. Then Paul speaks of the truth of the Gospel: "Was it by the works of the law that you received the Spirit of God, or was it by the hearing of faith? Even as Abraham believed God and it was accounted unto him for righteousness. As it is written in Habakkuk 2:4, "The just shall live by faith" (cf. Gal. 3:2, 6, 11). The just shall live by faith, not by law, not by ritual, not by ceremony, not by calendar, not by almanac, not by genuflexes, not by litany, not by feelings, not by speculation, not by philosophy, not by metaphysics. The just shall live by faith! Is not that a powerful monosyllabic sentence? "The just shall live by faith." It is a creative and liberating sentence, like that monosyllabic fiat from God, "Let there be light." So the monosyllable sentence, "The just shall live by faith." Oh, what a resounding text that is from Habakkuk 2:4! When Paul wrote the letter to the Roman church he used that text in Romans 1:17. The text is found again in Hebrews 10:38 and here it is in the Book of Galatians. As you know it was also the great text of the Reformation.

The Just Do Not Live by Feelings

"The just shall live by faith." Many of us would make it read, "The just shall live by feelings." By our feelings—when everything is calm, smooth, solubrious, felicitous, and happy for us, then we know we are in the will and favor of God. We are really blessed. We belong to the family and the household of faith. Everything is going our way. "I know I am saved because I am prosperous," we think. But when the way gets dark, when the winds get boisterous, when the waves are rolling high, when the night is black, and we cannot see the light, when the clouds are lowering and everything has fallen into despair, then we think that God does not love us anymore and we have lost our salvation. We say: "I am not really regenerated: I am just lost. I am just forgotten—the Lord does not even know I am here." We define God's attitude toward us by our feelings. We attach our salvation to our feelings. We say: "I am saved if I feel that I am saved. I am in God's good pleasure if everything is happy. But if it is not that way, then God has forsaken me and I am not a child of His at all. I have been forgotten." Listen, if you ever attach your salvation to your feelings and if you ever attach your religion to your feelings, you will be dragged to death by them. It is a miserable way to live. It is a dying life. It is a hand-to-mouth existence. It has no foundation in it, no substance, no assurance.

Dear me! The basis of my salvation is not in me, it is in God. The foundation of my hope is not in me, it is in Christ. If my salvation is in me and if it depends upon me, what shall I do? Faulty, frail, filled with mistake, error, sin, and finally fallen in senility, age, weakness, disease, and death, what shall I do? Incapable, unable, without strength, how can I save myself? As long as I look for the basis of my salvation in myself and in how I feel, I have no other destiny but one of abject, abysmal loss and despair. God help me and be merciful to me! And that is exactly and precisely the way that I am saved. Lord, Lord I cannot save myself—I am undone, I am weak, I face death. O God, be merciful to me! That is what saves me. It is casting myself upon God. It is looking to Christ. Salvation is in Him. Hope is in Him. It is not in us. When I come to Christ, He says: "I will in no wise cast out those who come to Me, who cast themselves upon Me. I give to them eternal life, and they shall never perish." Oh, I can wake up at 2:00 in the morning, at 4:00 in the morning, at twilight or at dawn or at the meridian strength of the sun, and the promise of Christ never changes. John 1:11 says, "He came unto his own, and his own received him not." John 1:12 says, "But as many as received him, to them gave he power to become the sons of God, even to them that believe on his name." That does not change. Lord, I have trusted Thee. I do believe in Thee. My hope is in Thee. And that is what saves me. O senseless, foolish, Galatians, who has bewitched you that you should turn aside from the faith and hope in Christ, and begin looking at yourself. The just shall live by feelings? No, never.

The Just Do Not Live by Speculation

Some of us would say the just live by speculation. What a frail, bruised reed to lean on, and what sand for foundation to build a house on! The just shall live by speculation, by philosophical metaphysics! The Bible speaks of repentance, faith, Christ, and the acceptance of the Lord. Some say, "I know that, but this is the way *I* think about it, and this is the way *I* look at it." And they propose to live by speculation, human reasoning, and philosophy. To my great sorrow of sorrows, no small part of the churches of Christ in the earth have done just that. They have turned aside from the evangelization of the world and the presentation of the Gospel, and they have given themselves to theological hair-splitting and all kinds of speculative metaphysical delineations, discussions, and declensions. In the first Christian centuries, when it looked as if the Christians were going to win the whole world to the faith, they turned aside and began in-fighting. One such altercation was the Arian controversy between Arius and Athanasius. Edward Gibbon said that they divided the entire civilized world over a Greek iota. Arius said that Christ was *homoiousios* and Athanasius said that Christ was *homöousios*. Someone came to me one time and said, "Well, do you think it is immaterial whether he was *homoiousios* (of like substance) or *homöousios* (of the same substance)?" I said: "Yes, it makes a difference. But the biggest difference is that when we get to looking at those things and start fighting one another, what happens to us is that we forget the evangelization of the world." That is exactly what happened to the Christian faith. In three centuries they had literally won the civilized world. Then they stopped there in the Graeco-Roman Empire. The great masses of the east, west, north, and south; Africa, northern Europe, India, China, Japan, all of them were forgotten and for the most part are still forgotten today. The just shall live by speculation, by metaphysics, by philosophy? No! Never!

The Just Do Not Live by Worldly Prudence

The just shall live by prudence, by smartness, by shrewdness? The world says that is the way to get along. You do not need to pray, you do not need God. You do not need religion, you do not need the church, you do not need worship. All you need is shrewdness, astuteness, and smartness and you will get places in this world. The just shall live by prudence.

Do you remember Lot whose herdsmen began to war with the herdsmen of Abraham because the land was not able to contain their vast, increasing herds and flocks? Abraham said to his nephew, Lot: "Let there be no strife between your people and my people, your herdsmen and my herdsmen. The land is before you. You choose what you think is best for you, and what is remaining to me I shall accept as under God. You make the choice." Lot stood on the edge of the height of the mountain and looked at the well-watered plains that lay like an emerald carpet before him. He looked upon the thriving, merchandising, flourishing cities of Sodom and Gomorrah, and he turned to his uncle, the old patriarch Abraham, and said, "If I have my choice I will choose the well-watered plains, and the teeming city life of Sodom and Gomorrah." Shrewd? Yes! Smart? Yes! Wise in this world? Yes! Look at those plains with the flowing streams, look at those fields so green, look at those cities teeming with market possibilities. Prudence? The just shall live by prudence, smartness? "And Lot pitched his tent toward Sodom." They elected him mayor. He sat at the gate and he was prosperous. But Abraham, up there in those barren, rocky mountains, was walking with God, close to the heart of the Almighty. Abraham—believing, trusting, worshiping, loving, serving God. For the just shall live by trust, by faith, by commitment, by prayer, by loving Jehovah Lord.

Teach us, Master, Thy will and way—to love Thee, to trust Thee, to commit our way unto Thee, asking God to bless us and to save us. If there are any rites, they are secondary, if there are any rituals, they are thirdary. If there are any ceremonies, they are fourthdary. If there are any other laws to keep, they are sixthdary. If there is anything else in religion it is seventhdary, eighthdary, or ninth or no dary at all. But the primary, the fundamental, the great commitment is our personal confrontation with God, keeping Him central, loving the Lord, worshiping Him, trusting in Him. "O foolish Galatians, who hath bewitched you?" Come back to the faith, come back to Jesus. For the just shall live by their trust in God.

CHAPTER 8

CHRIST OUR REDEEMER

> For as many as are of the works of the law are under the curse: for it is written, Cursed is every one that continueth not in all things which are written in the book of the law to do them.
>
> Christ hath redeemed us from the curse of the law, being made a curse for us: for it is written, Cursed is every one that hangeth on a tree:
>
> That the blessing of Abraham might come on the Gentiles through Jesus Christ; that we might receive the promise of the Spirit through faith." (Gal. 3:10, 13, 14)

In our study of the Book of Galatians we are in the third chapter and this chapter in our book is an exposition of verses 10, 13, and 14. This is verse 10: "For as many as are of the works of the law are under the curse: for it is written, Cursed is every one that continueth not in all things which are written in the book of the law to do them." Now verses 13 and 14: "Christ hath redeemed us from the curse of the law, being made a curse for us: . . . That the blessing of Abraham might come on the Gentiles through Jesus Christ; that we might receive the promise of the Spirit through faith."

Would you not think that the words in verse 10 comprise an astonishing observation? "As many as are of the works of the law are under the curse. . . ." When a man tries to save himself by doing good, by keeping laws and commandments, he is cursed in his attempts. Such a position is in direct opposition to the view taken by the world and by all other systems of religion. You would almost think that religion would address itself to the soul of a man and say: "You ought to do good. Do this and thou shalt live. Obey these commandments and you will have eternal life." But the revelation here in the Word of God says just the opposite. "As many as are of the works of the law are under the curse: for it is written, Cursed is every one that continueth not in all things which are written in the book of the law to do them."

The giving of the law was in itself an awesome and terrible sight. Mount Sinai burned with fire; it was an upheaval of thunder and lightning. The giving of the law was accompanied by the blast of a terrible trumpet. It sounded like the day of doom, like the day of damnation and destruction. The Scriptures say that the people feared that blasting of the trumpet more than they did the fury of flame, fire, thunder, smoke, and lightning. So awesome and terrible was the sight that even Moses said, "I do exceedingly fear and quake." It was such a fearful time that if a beast or man touched the mount of Sinai he should die immediately, thrust through with a dart.

The awesomeness of that drama was accompanied by the laws written on tables of stone. Those laws are impersonal and universally applicable. They are written on rock—heavy rocks that crush us, grind us into the dust. "Cursed is everyone that continueth not in all things which are written in the book of the law to do them."

The Law With Its Condemnation and Judgment

For a man to seek to be saved by the works of the law is to find himself damned, cursed, judged before he begins. The law is impersonal. It has no favorites. Whoever we are, when we do not continue in the law to keep it, the moment we break it, that moment we fall into judgment and damnation. A man might keep ninety-nine laws and fail in the last one. He might keep 99 percent of the law but if he fails in that final 1 percent he falls into condemnation and judgment. "Cursed is every one that continueth not in all things which are written in the book of the law to do them." There is no exception. The law is impersonal and universally applicable.

The sinful woman who came off the street when Jesus was a guest at dinner with Simon the Pharisee and bathed His feet with her tears, anointed Him with spikenard of ointment, and dried His feet with the hairs of her head—the law says that she is to be stoned (Luke 7:36-50). Mercy and grace are something else, but the law says that she is to be taken outside of the city and stoned until she dies. But not only is that law applicable to a malefactor, to a felon, or to a murderer, to a vile sinner, but it is applicable to all of us, for there is no exception. The trail of the serpent is everywhere in the earth. There is poison that has entered the fountain of our hearts. There is a black drop that courses through all our veins. Without rank, without station, without anything to commend us to God, we are naked, fallen, sinful, and lost before Him. For us to try to cover ourselves by our self-righteousness is to clothe ourselves in garments of filth and dirt. For one to protect himself and to shield himself from the judgment of God is as though one were to seek to hide himself behind a web of spider material—thin, fragile, frail. It is cut through with the sword of the law.

"Cursed is every one that continueth not in all things which are written in the book of the law to do them." If we try to commend ourselves to God by works of righteousness, we immediately fall into judgment because our works are not all righteous. Our lives are not all pure. Our hearts are not all clean. There is sin, dereliction, and mistake in all of us. In that moment that we do wrong, that moment we are cursed. "Cursed is everyone that continueth not in all things which are written in the law to do them."

The working out of that judgment is as awesome and as terrible as the giving of the law itself. The working out of that judgment is death in this physical frame. Sin is universal, therefore death is universal. It comes to you some day, somewhere, sometime. "The soul that sinneth, it shall die" (Ezek. 18:4). "The wages of sin is death" (Rom. 6:23). "Cursed is every one that continueth not in all things which are written in the book of the law to do them." That curse destroys in an awesome way all of our lives. We die physically. This body, this house in which I live, is judged. I would not die if I had not sinned. A sign of the weakness and the lostness of our human nature is found in the universal sign of our dying.

But not only in this physical frame do we die. We also die spiritually. We die a second death. We die in an eternal separation from God. "Cursed, judged, damned is everyone that continueth not in all things which are written in the book of the law to do them." That no man is justified by the law in the sight of God is evident. If we were brought into the presence of God one at a time, it is evident that there would not be one of us today, or in the congregation that worshiped in this place before us, nor in the generation that shall follow us, who could stand in the divine presence of God and say: "I am above the judgment of those iron commandments. I am pure, I am holy, I shall not die." His very words would mock him, and his own experience would condemn him. "Cursed is every one that continueth not in all things which are written in the book of the law to do them."

How God Can Be Just and Yet Forgive the Sinner

Then how is it that we could ever be saved? Sinners as we are, cursed as we are, judged as we are, damned as we are, dying as we are, how could we ever be saved? This is the Gospel of the grace of the Son of God. For the law came through Moses (judgment is one thing) but grace, truth, forgiveness, and salvation—that is another thing. Mercy is still another thing. For the law came through Moses, but mercy, grace, truth, and forgiveness came through Jesus Christ (cf. John 1:17). "Christ hath redeemed us from the curse of the law, being made a curse for us . . . that we might receive the promise of the Spirit through faith."

The salvation of fallen man poses a problem that was difficult even for God. How does God honor the law, and at the same time forgive a sinner? In answer, one says God could overlook the sin, forget it, blind His eyes to it. God writes the law on tables of stone, and He reveals it by divine revelation both in the human heart (all of us are sensitive to it) and He reveals it also in the divine Word. But having revealed it and having written it and having presented it and having opened it by revelation for our eyes to see it and our hearts to feel it, why, then, does not God shut His eyes to it? Why does He not overlook it? Such an action on the part of God would make a mockery of the divine legislation. It would be to dishonor His law, and God does not dishonor His law. If God, then, does not overlook His law, dishonor His law, forget

His law, then how can God save us? For we are sinners, damned, lost, and judged, "Cursed is every one that continueth not in all things which are written in the book of the law to do them." How is God just and at the same time the justifier of the ungodly?

God cannot overlook his laws. He does not. He will not. His law will be honored. It is written in the fourteenth chapter of the Book of Numbers, that God will by no means clear the guilty, but will visit the sins of the fathers upon the children to the third and the fourth generations. (See v. 18.) That is God. He honors His law. Then, how can God save us? How can He be just, right, and at the same time justify the ungodly, justify a sinner? This is the Gospel. "Christ hath redeemed us from the curse of the law, being made a curse for us. . . ." The original words are *huper hemon,* "in our behalf," "in our stead," "for us." God's law is to be satisfied, it is to be honored. There will be blood for blood, there will be stroke for stroke, there will be judgment for judgment, there will be punishment for punishment. There will be an eye for an eye, and a tooth for a tooth. The sword of the law will be satisfied. But this is the Gospel of the grace of the Son of God, that Christ was made accursed, He was judged, He was damned, He was condemned—*huper hemon,* "in our stead." He took our place for us.

All of the Old Testament sacrificial systems typified that substitution. Every lamb that was slain and whose blood was poured out, every offering on that flaming, brazen fire, every Day of Atonement, every Yom Kippur, every sprinkling of the blood between the cherubim, every priest who ever sacrificed before God, typified that great revelation of substitution. "He died in our stead." When the worshiper came with his offering, he took the sacrificial animal and put his hands on its head, confessed there his sins and the animal was slain with its blood poured out at the base of the altar. Why? By putting his hands on the head of the animal, he identified himself with the lamb or with the bullock, and when the animal was slain, it was as though he, the worshiper, had been slain. It was a substitutionary sacrifice. That is the Gospel. "Christ hath redeemed us from the curse of the law, being made a curse for us. . . ." There is in Christ an actual substitution. This is not a metaphor or simile. This is not poetry or fiction. This is· not imagination. This is an actual substitution. God took Christ, His only begotten Son, and delivered Him to our judgment and to our death, damnation, and cursing. He received in His own body the stab and the curse and the judgment. He died in our stead.

Christ Jesus Our Actual Substitute

That marvelous Gospel is presented in the same language in 2 Corinthians 5:21: "For he hath made him to be sin for us, who knew no sin; that we might be made the righteousness of God in him." God hath made Him to be sin *for us, huper hemon,* the identical words in the text here in Galatians 3:13. "Christ hath redeemed us from the curse of the law, being made a curse for us—*huper hemon.*" God made Christ Jesus that curse for us. By nature, by divine life He was not cursed. He was spotless. He was pure. He was sinless. He did not have to die. But God made Him to be sin, *huper hemon,* "in our stead." God made Him accursed that we might be made the righteousness of God in Him. That is, He actually took our place of judgment, dying in our stead. When you look at the cross and the Lord dying on it, that is you dying. That is you cursed. That is you judged. And if someone were to ask how could one be so meritorious and virtuous that He could die for all of us, the answer lies in the dignity, in the divinity, in the deity of His person. Christ is able to bear the judgment for all of us because He is God manifest in the flesh. So superlative is the merit of His life that His soul's agony is efficacious to the saving of us all.

Let us look again upon that actual substitution. *Huper hemon,* made a curse "instead of us," made sin "instead of us." The law did Christ fully saitsfy, judgment for judgment, blood for blood, damnation for damnation. All of our sin and its consequent damnation did He take there in His own body on the tree. The substitution was vividly actual.

For illustration, there are several things that sin does, that breaking of the law does. First, sin separates. It will separate between a man and God. It did so in the Garden of Eden. When Adam, who had been in fellowship with the Lord, talking with Him face to face, transgressed God's commandment, he hid himself. When he heard the voice of the Lord God walking in the garden in the cool of the day, he could not be found. God said, "Adam, Adam, where art thou?" And the fallen man replied, "I have hid myself." Thus it was that Christ our Savior, who became our sin, was separated from God on the cross. He cried, "My God, my God, why hast thou forsaken me?" Sin separated the dying Son from the Holy Father. The Gospel tells us why: The Son was dying in our stead. Sin separates and Christ was separated from God. He was forsaken.

A second thing, sin deprives. Sin robs. It leaves us naked, wretched, and lost. Look at Jesus in His actual substitution for us. The artists are most kind. I have never seen a picture of Jesus, dying on the cross, but that the artist somehow managed some piece of clothing to cover His nakedness. But Jesus did not die clothed. He died stripped. He died naked. He had five pieces of clothing. To the quaternion of soldiers, they gave one piece to one, one to the other, a third to the other, and a fourth, to another, but the seamless garment they said should not be divided. "Let us not tear it or rend it; let us cast lots for it." And at the foot of the cross, beneath the naked, dying body of our Lord, they cast lots for which one of the quaternion would take it. (See Matthew 27:35.) Sin deprives. The soldiers took away everything He had, even His clothing.

Sin causes suffering and pain. Christ our substitute so suffered for us. God shall see of the travail of His soul and shall be satisfied (Isa. 53:11). His sweat was as if it were great drops of blood falling to the ground (Luke 22:44). He suffered. There is no execution ever devised by the cruel heart of man that equals in pain and agony the Roman system of execution, namely, nailing to a cross. There were times when the one executed lingered for days in unspeakable agony. He died in pain, in sobs, in cries, and in tears.

And last, sin kills. Christ our actual substitute so died for us. He was numbered among the transgressors as one of us, and for our sins He bowed His head and said, "Father, into thy hands I commend my spirit." Thus He bowed His head and died. I am illustrating here that in Christ there is an actual substitution. The teaching of the substitutionary sacrifice of Christ is not a figment of the imagination, it is not fictional. Christ died actually, *huper hemon,* "in our stead." He made for us an actual atonement. "All we like sheep have gone astray; we have turned every one to his own way; and the LORD hath laid on him the iniquity of us all. But he was wounded for our transgressions, he was bruised for our iniquities: the chastisement of our peace was upon him; and with his stripes we are healed" (Isa. 53:6, 5). There is an actual substitution. "Cursed is every one that continueth not in all things which are written in the book of the law to do them." We are cursed! "But Christ hath redeemed us from the curse of the law, being made a curse for us"—*huper hemon*—"in our stead." In Christ there is an actual substitution: the curse and the judgment came upon Him and the blessings of faith and salvation come upon us. We who receive the Lord and the promises of the Spirit through faith, finding ourselves unable, lost, condemned, judged, cursed (for all of us have sinned and all of us are under the curse) have now been forgiven, justified, saved forever, delivered from the condemnation and judgment upon our transgressions.

Christ in the fullness of time came to this earth, born of a woman, made under the law that He might redeem us from the curse of the law. He was made a curse for us that He might redeem us to God, that we might have the blessings of the Lord through faith in Him. When I accept the Lord, when I trust in the Lord, when I believe in the Lord, all that the Lord is, is mine, as all I am becomes His. There are two sides to that substitutionary death. If our Lord took my place, if He died *huper hemon,* "in my stead," if He took my place, then the other side of the Gospel is that I have His place. I take His life, I take His robes of righteousness. If He takes my filthy rags, then I have His beautiful garments, pure and white, washed in the blood of the Lamb. I lay down my bondage, He takes it. I pick up His liberty—that is mine. He died for me, and I live in Him. What of me, I lay down and Christ takes that. What of Christ, I pick up and that is mine. If He died for me and my sin, then what is of Christ is mine. We just exchange places. He died for me. I live because of Him. He took my sins, my curse, my damnation, and my judgment. I have His mercy, forgiveness, and life—now and forever. This is the wonderful Gospel, the Good News of the Son of God.

The Marvel and Glory of Our Salvation

Let us look more closely and joyously at that gift of God in Christ Jesus. Our salvation, for one thing, is always instantaneous. The gift is always immediate. The Gospel is, "Look and live, wash and be clean, believe and be saved." There may be many things that lead up to it. There may be the hearing of the Word, the preaching of the Gospel, prayer, and sometimes agony of spirit, civil war in the soul, but when it comes, always that glorous gift of redemption is instantaneous. The entire work of our Lord is like that. When He saw the paralytic He said, "Arise, take up your bed and walk." And the man did just that —he arose and walked immediately. He said to the man whose ears were closed and deaf, "*Ephphatha,*" and immediately his ears were opened. He said to the raging storm, "Be still," and it was quiet. He said to Jairus' daughter, "*Talitha cumi,*" "Damsel, arise," and immediately she was raised from the dead. That is the way salvation comes to us. It is immediate. It is instantaneous.

> There is a life for a look at the crucified One,
> There is life at this moment for thee—
> Then look, sinner, look unto Him and be saved,
> Unto Him who was nailed to the tree.
>
> I've a message from the Lord, hallelujah,
> It is only that you "look and live."
> Look and live, my brother, live!
> Look to Jesus now and live;
> 'Tis recorded in His Word, hallelujah!
> It is only that you "look and live."

Second, salvation is absolutely complete. It is all-sufficient and all-adequate. It needs, it lacks nothing else. All of the waters of Neptune's ocean could not wash the stain of sin out of our souls. All the sweet spices and perfumes of Arabia could not cover over the guilt of our sin. But the blood of Jesus Christ is all-sufficient, it is complete, it is adequate. It is not possible for Christ to forget some of our sins but not others. God does not forgive us of only present sin, but also those we should commit tomorrow. He is able to forgive *all* our sins.

His atoning grace is complete, all-sufficient, all-adequate. It covers the entire expanse of the wrong and ruin of our lives. Even in death He is able to raise us up.

And last, salvation is irrevocable. When God gives us Himself, He does not take Himself back. When God bestows upon us salvation, He does not let us fall into the abyss and into hell. His merciful gift of life is irrevocable, it is a forever, it is now and in the world that is to come. We should sing these words with fervor, zeal and faith,

> The soul that on Jesus hath leaned for repose,
> I will not, I will not desert to his foes;
> That soul, though all hell should endeavor to shake,
> I'll never, no never, no never forsake!

Who shall add anything to the charge of God's elect? It is God that justified us. "For I am persuaded, that neither death, nor life, nor angels, nor principalities, nor powers, nor things present, nor things to come, nor height, nor depth, nor any other creature shall be able to separate us from the love of God, which is in Christ Jesus our Lord" (Rom. 8:38, 39). It is a forever gift.

"As many as are of the works of the law are under the curse: for it is written, Cursed is every one that continueth not in all things which are written in the book of the law to do them." But, "Christ hath redeemed us from the curse of the law, being made a curse for us (*huper hemon,* "in our stead") that we might be the righteousness of God in him." When I accept Christ, it is done. The great transaction is done I take it, when I trust him, when I believe in Him, when I open my heart to Him—the great transaction is done. God does it. It is a miracle of heaven. "Lord, this hast Thou done for me, and this, Lord, shall I do for Thee. I give Thee my heart and my life in faith, in trust, in belief, in acceptance, and in love—now and forever."

Chapter 9

THE CURSE AND THE TREE

> But that no man is justified by the law in the sight of God, it is evident: for, The just shall live by faith.
>
> And the law is not of faith: but, The man that doeth them shall live in them.
>
> Christ hath redeemed us from the curse of the law, being made a curse for us: for it is written, Cursed is every one that hangeth on a tree:
>
> That the blessing of Abraham might come on the Gentiles through Jesus Christ; that we might receive the promise of the Spirit through faith. (Gal. 3:11-14)

The title of this chapter is "The Curse and the Tree." As a background I read from the Book of Deuteronomy the verse that Paul will quote in the passage that is our Galatian text. In Deuteronomy 21 Moses concludes that chapter with these words: "And if a man have committed a sin worthy of death, and he be to be put to death, and thou hang him on a tree: His body shall not remain all night upon the tree, but thou shalt in any wise bury him that day; (for he that is hanged is accursed of God;) that thy land be not defiled, which the Lord thy God giveth thee for an inheritance" (vv. 22, 23). That verse, "for he that is hanged is accursed of God," is also found in the text in Galatians 3: "For as many as are of the works of the law are under the curse: for it is written, Cursed is every one that continueth not in all things which are written in the book of the law to do them. But that no man is justified by the law in the sight of God, it is evident: for, The just shall live by faith. And the law is not of faith: but, The man that doeth them shall live in them. Christ hath redeemed us from the curse of the law, being made a curse for us: for it is written, [and the apostle quotes that passage from Deut. 21:23] Cursed is every one that hangeth on a tree: That the blessing of Abraham might come on the Gentiles through Jesus Christ; that we might receive the promise of the Spirit through faith" (Gal. 3:9-14).

The Beautiful Tree and the Beautiful Life

Among the trees that grew around Jerusalem in the days of Caiaphas the high priest was one that was tall and towering, a beautiful and magnificent specimen of God's handiwork, a marvelous and glorious tree. But debased, degraded, and cruel men took that beautiful tree in hand and cut it down. They denuded it; they defoliated it of its beautiful leaves. They tore off its branches, they ripped off its bark, they cut its body in two and they made of it a harsh, rude, cruel, cross. They prepared it for the execution of a traitor, a malefactor, an enemy of the people. Death by crucifixion was the hard, crude, cruel way of punishment on the part of the Roman government.

Among the men who lived in the days of Pontius Pilate, there was one man who towered above all others. He was the Son of God, holy, pure, heavenly, perfect in His life, merciful, compassionate, unselfish, giving Himself for those who needed the healing touch and the saving presence of God. Debased, degraded, cruel, and bloodthirsty men took Him and stripped Him of His glory. They divided among themselves His garments, even casting lots for His seamless robe. They took His naked body and nailed Him to that cross, and both of them were lifted up above the earth and beneath the sky: that man and that tree—both of them denuded, debased, degraded. They dug a hole in the earth and plunged one end of that tree down in the dirt. The other end reached up toward God in heaven. The outstretched crossbeams turned toward the east and the west, as far as the east and the west do go. Held against the tree was the agonizing, suffering, naked, dying Son of God.

After the agony was over, men separated the dead man from the dead wood, but inseparable forever in memory and in mind, in thought and in history, is that man and that tree, that Christ and that cross. And that hole in the ground in which they placed that tree became the pivot around which swings the destiny of the civilized world. In the power and in the glory of God, that dead man lives again, raised from among those who have fallen into the arms of corruption and decay. The glad announcement to the disciples was, "He is alive!" The glorious good news like liquid fire spread from heart to heart, mouth to mouth, tongue to tongue, and word to word until it filled all Jerusalem, spilled over into Judaea and Samaria, sped along the Roman roads around the Mediterranean, and turned the idolatrous civilization of the dead, cold Roman world into a living hope and into a new course. Christ, the Son of God, who died on the tree, is alive again!

And that tree began to grow. It sent down deep roots into the heart of the earth. Those roots pierced through fire, through flood, through hearts, through souls, through time, through centuries, through cultures, and through civilization. It bear twelve manner of fruit and yielded its fruit every month. And the leaves of the tree are for the healing of the nations. The tree of life in the Garden of Eden, the tree of life in the paradise of God in heaven, is none other than that tree that was so cruelly cut down and made into the form of a rude and rugged cross.

The Glory of God in the Cross of Christ

In the power of God, in an astonishing, miraculous intervention from heaven, the coarse cross with its ugliness, its shame, its horror, and its agony has been turned into beauty, into glory, into hope, and in salvation. Ugliness into beauty! What could have been more disdainful to taste and to cultured sensitivity than two cross-ties with the beams placed diametrically opposite one another. In the Coliseum in Rome for years has stood a rugged cross where the Christians were martyred to appease bloodthirsty throngs. Thinking of the cross as a horrible instrument of execution, I cannot but be overwhelmed by the miracle from heaven and the intervention from God that the Apostle Paul should be able to say in the last chapter of this book, "God forbid that I should glory, save in the cross of our Lord Jesus Christ." The cross has become in poetry, in art, in literature, in song, and in sermon glorified and immortalized. That tree, that cross has come to symbolize the Son of God who was nailed to it and died on it. Beautiful temples of worship all over this earth have been built in the form of that cross with the central nave and the transcepts on either side. Beahtiful gems, precious stones have been cut in the form of that cross. Silver has been chased and gold fashioned in the form of that cross. And on countless numbers of shrines of intercession will one find that tree lifted high, pointing toward heaven as the hope of man in God who so loved us that He sent His Son to die for us.

From Hong Kong one time I went to Macao, the Portuguese Colony now under the surveillance of Red China. A most impressive sight can be looked upon there. On a high hill with tremendous flights of steps leading up to it from the heart of the city is what remains of Saint Paul's Cathedral. All that is left is the facade of the church and on top of it a towering cross. In a violent earthquake accompanied by fire, hurricane, and storm, the entire church was destroyed, but there remained that front wall with the cross rising upon the pinnacle. John Bowring (born in 1792, died in 1872) visited Macao and was so impressed by the spectacular sight of the façade of that church with the cross at the zenith that he wrote the beautiful hymn, "In the Cross of Christ I Glory."

In the cross of Christ I glory,
Tow'ring o'er the wrecks of time;
All the light of sacred story
Gathers round its head sublime.

Bane and blessing, pain and pleasure,
By the cross are sanctified;
Peace is there that knows no measure,
Joys that thro' all time abide.

Ugliness into beauty, and the curse into a blessing this God has done for us. "Christ hath redeemed us from the curse of the law, being made a curse for us: for it is written, Cursed is every one that hangeth on a tree: That the blessing of Abraham might come on the Gentiles through Jesus Christ; that we might receive the promise of the Spirit through faith" (Gal. 3:13, 14).

What hath God wrought with that tree so cut down, so cut through, used for such ugly and inhuman purposes! Through the cross has come to us our hope of salvation. As Paul wrote in the first chapter of 1 Corinthians, "But we preach Christ crucified [Christ nailed to a tree, Christ dying in sobs and tears, Christ bathed in His own blood], unto the Jews a *skandalon* [translated 'a stumbling block']" (v. 23). How could a man in his right mind glorify a gallows, an electric chair, a cross, the instrument of the cruelest execution ever devised by the mind of men? "To the Jews a *skandalon,* to the Greeks, *morian* [translated 'foolishness,' moronic, idiocy]. . . ." How could a man like Paul who calls himself rational and reasonable stand in the presence of philosophers trained in universities like those at Athens and proclaim salvation through the cross, through the execution of a man? But the apostle is emphatic, avowing that to us who are saved, the Son of God is Christ crucified, Christ the power of God, Christ the love of God, Christ the wisdom of God (cf. 1 Cor. 1:24). As music finds expression through an instrument and as electricity finds its expression through lines, cables, and wires, so does the spiritual power of God find its outreach, its blessing, its expression in the cross of Jesus Christ. Mediated to us is the presence, the love, the saving grace of God in that tree so cruelly cut down.

Deliverance and Blessing in the Cross of Christ

The cross is the aegis and the sign of our freedom, our liberty, and our deliverance through the centuries. Since the creation, men have been oppressed by darkness, by ignorance, by the fear of death, by the weight of sin and superstition. But the Lord said in the eighth chapter of the Book of John, "And ye shall know the truth, and the truth shall make you free" (v. 32). Then in the fourteenth chapter of the same gospel, Jesus said, "I am the way, the truth, and the life." (v. 6). This liberty and this freedom have come to us in the cross of the Son of God. Victor Hugo, delivering an address at the planting of the Liberty Tree in Paris, said, "The first tree of liberty was planted by God Himself on Golgotha." Remembering the gladiatorial combats that stained the sandy floor of the Coliseum with rich, red, human blood, I realize that in the cross came deliverance, liberty, and freedom to the slaves who were slain. In that cross came protection for the captives. In that cross came elevation for womanhood. In that cross came ministries to blessed, innocent children. In that cross came education for the darkened mind. In that cross came care for the sick and the needy. Wherever the cross of Christ has been raised, wherever that tree has been lifted up, there one will find the orphans' home, the hospital, the school, and the church with its spire pointing men to heaven.

In the cross is mediated to us the transforming power of Christ, God's only Son. Out of its darkness came light; out of its death came life; and out of its sufferings came salvation. There were three years of His ministry, three dark hours when the sun refused to shine as He died, and three days in the cold, dark tomb, and then glory, glory, glory! He is raised from the dead and the news of His transforming, changing, regenerating power has made new men. Simon Peter is a coward no more. The cowering disciples who crawled in eleven shadows hiding from the face of Jerusalem are bold like lions. They are standing and spreading abroad the glorious news that Christ is raised from the dead and in Him there is power—power to live, power to rise from the grave, power to seek God's face. These followers of Christ are new people, they are new men. And that same transforming power touched the entire Graeco-Roman world. The Christian disciples were the heralds and the harbingers of the new civilization. Wherever the message has gone into any foreign land and to any darkened country, there has it spread light, glory, triumph, and victory. That transforming power of the cross has reached now, even to us in our lives, in our hearts, in our homes where we live. In Him we are new people. The believer is a new creation, he is something else, he is gloriously changed by the power of the Gospel in the preaching of the cross.

There is an unusual story illustrating the transforming power of the grace of God in Christ Jesus. There was a man who was a drunkard. He took his paycheck and spent it on alcohol. He lived in the dirt and vomit of the gutter. His children were ragged and hungry; his wife was neglected and starved; his home was a shambles. Men came and repossessed his furniture and the family lived in an open, barren house. In the kind and merciful providences of God, the transforming power of the cross of Christ reached down to this drunkard and he became a new man, a regenerated man. The furniture was returned to the home, the payments on the mortgage continued, and there was born a new life and a new day. One day one of his old cronies began to ridicule him about becoming a Christian and about believing the Bible. One of the critic's barbs of sarcasm and ridicule concerned something that Jesus did in His miraculous power—turning water into wine. That old crony sarcastically said to this regenerated believer, "Do you mean to tell me that you believe that stuff in the Bible? Take that story of the Lord changing water into wine, do you believe such a thing as that?" And the man replied: "Sir, I am no theologian. I'm an unlettered and an uneducated man and I am not able to answer. I don't know how He did it. All I know is this: that in my life he changed beer into furniture, whiskey into mortgage payments, and drunkenness into the worship of God, and that is good enough for me!"

The concluding sentence of that man's testimony, "and that is good enough for me," has rung in my heart and in my mind. All the days of my conscious life I have studied the Bible. As a boy I did so. I did so in college, in the seminary, in graduate work. And yet after the passing of a life and a generation, I humbly but honestly confess there are ten thousand things about the aeons and the ages past that I do not understand. There are other ten thousand things about the centuries and the millennia of the future that I do not understand. There are no less than ten thousand things of the miraculous present around me and above me that I do not understand. My finite mind is not able to enter into the infinitude of the mysteries of God. All I know is this: aboundingly I see God's grace around me, and that is good enough for me. I see the goodness of God working in the lives of our children, and that is good enough for me. I see the blessing and grace of God in the recreation of men and women, and that is good enough for me. I see the hope of heaven in the faces of those who are facing inevitable death, and that is good enough for me. And I feel in my own soul the hope of heaven in my heart beyond the days of the pilgrimage of this life when the Lord shall open the doors and the vistas of glory, and that is good enough for me. All the grace and graciousness and goodness of God in Christ Jesus is given to us immortalized, glorified forever in that tree and in that Man, in that cross, and in that Christ. And that is good enough for me!

Chapter 10

THE BROKEN LAW

> Wherefore then serveth the law? It was added because of transgressions, till the seed should come to whom the promise was made; and it was ordained by angels in the hand of a mediator.
>
> Now a mediator is not a mediator of one, but God is one.
>
> Is the law then against the promises of God? God forbid: for if there had been a law given which could have given life, verily righteousness should have been by the law.
>
> But the scripture hath concluded all under sin, that the promise by faith of Jesus Christ might be given to them that believe. (Gal. 3:19-22)

The gist of the sermon is "Why the Law?" As a background for the message we read the context in Galatians 3. "Brethren, I speak after the manner of men; Though it be but a man's covenant, yet if it be confirmed, no man disannulleth, or addeth thereto. Now to Abraham and his seed were the promises made. He saith not, And to seeds, as of many; but as of one, And to thy seed, which is Christ. And this I say, that the covenant, that was confirmed before of God in Christ, the law, which was four hundred and thirty years after, cannot disannul, that it should make the promise of none effect. For if the inheritance be of the law, it is no more of promise: but God gave it to Abraham by promise. Wherefore then serveth the law? It was added because of transgressions, till the seed should come to whom the promise was made; and it was ordained by angels in the hand of a mediator. Is the law then against the promises of God? God forbid: for if there had been a law given which could have given life, verily righteousness should have been by the law. But the scripture hath concluded all under sin, that the promise by faith of Jesus Christ might be given to them that believe" (vv. 15-19, 21, 22).

The text is verse 19, which, in the King James Version, reads, "Wherefore then serveth the law?" Notice that the word "serveth" is in italics; that is, it is not in the original language. It was added to make it clearer when it was translated into English. The question is *Ti houn ho nomos; ti*—"why," *houn*—"therefore," *ho nomos*—"the law," "Why, then, the law?" The reason that Paul asks the question is because of what he has said in the entire chapter preceding. For example, in verse 17 he says that the promise antedated the law by four hundred thirty years. God gave to Abraham and to his descendants a way of salvation that was four hundred thirty years before the law was given. Now in the eleventh verse of chapter three he says, "No man is justified by the law in the sight of God," and for substantiating evidence he quotes the famous verse in Habakkuk, "The just shall live by faith" (2:4). Not by the law, but by the mercy, forgiveness, and goodness of God we are saved. The apostle further adds in the sixth through the eighth verses of the same chapter that all of us (Old Testament saints as well as New Tetsament saints) are saved by grace and not by the law, even as Abraham believed God, he trusted in God, and his trust was accounted for righteousness. "Therefore they that are of faith, these are the children of Abraham, the children of the promise" (cf. Gal. 3:7, 29). In the fifth verse of the third chapter the apostle said that we receive the Spirit, the Holy Spirit of God, not by the works of the law but by the hearing of faith. Having said all of those things, naturally, it brought up the question, the rhetorical one that is asked in the nineteenth verse which is our text, "*Ti* (why) *houn* (therefore)"—since all of these things are true, since we are not saved by the law, we are not justified by the law, since the Spirit of God is not given us by observing laws, commandments, statutes, judgments, rites, and rituals—since all of these things were true four hundred years before the law was given (God saved Abraham and his descendants by faith, by trust), then why the law? Why was the law given?

One might suppose that the law was incidental, that God

gave the law as an afterthought, that it is not dynamic, central, and primary. One might suppose that it is peripheral, almost incidental. No, that is not true, for in the Old Testament there is not anything that is presented that has in it the awesome, dramatic meaning like the giving of the law. Nor is there anything that Israel ever did that was so binding in covenant sanctification as the ratifying of the law.

The Dramatic Story of the Giving of the Law

The story is told in Exodus 19 and in the following chapters. Moses is introduced in Exodus 2. For forty years he was in Egypt, the son of Pharaoh's daughter, the heir-apparent to the throne. He was trained in all the art, wisdom, science, and knowledge of Egyptian culture. Then for forty years, following his training in Egypt, he was on the backside of the desert, in the school of God at Mount Sinai. After the exodus of the Israelites, Moses brought the people of God across the Red Sea into the Sinaitic Peninsula and there in a great plain about two miles long and a fourth of a mile wide (the plain leading up to that jagged, rugged mountain peak called Sinai, which is about six thousand five hundred feet high)—in that holy place and on that holy ground where the bush in the years before had burned unconsumed, God told Moses that He would come down and speak face to face with the people.

> And Moses went up unto God, and the LORD called unto him out of the mountain, saying, Thus shalt thou say to the house of Jacob, and tell the children of Israel;
>
> Ye have seen what I did unto the Egyptians, and how I bare you on eagles' wings, and brought you unto myself.
>
> Now therefore, if ye will obey my voice indeed, and keep my covenant, then ye shall be a peculiar treasure unto me above all people: for all the earth is mine:
>
> And ye shall be unto me a kingdom of priests, and an holy nation. These are the words which thou shalt speak unto the children of Israel.
>
> And Moses came and called for the elders of the people, and laid before their faces all these words which the LORD commanded him.
>
> And all the people answered together, and said, All that the LORD hath spoken we will do. And Moses returned the words of the people unto the LORD.
>
> And the LORD said unto Moses, Lo, I come unto thee in a thick cloud, that the people may hear when I speak with thee,

> and believe thee for ever. And Moses told the words of the people unto the LORD.
>
> And the LORD said unto Moses, Go unto the people, and sanctify them to-day and to-morrow, and let them wash their clothes.
>
> And be ready against the third day: for the third day the LORD will come down in the sight of all the people upon Mount Sinai.
>
> And thou shalt set bounds unto the people round about, saying, Take heed to yourselves, that ye go not up into the mount, or touch the border of it: whosoever toucheth the mount shall be surely put to death (Exod. 19:3-12).

Thus Moses gathered the people on the third day and they all stood in the presence of almighty God, ready to receive His laws, His commandments, His statutes, and judgments. On the third day, beginning in the morning, there were thunders, lightnings, a thick cloud, and then the sounding of the trumpet, not with human lips, but like the sound of the trumpet at the Judgment Day when God will raise the dead. Mount Sinai smoked like a furnace. The great mountain shook as the staggering of an addled man. The voice of the trumpet sounded long and waxed louder and louder, and the people were terrified at the awesome sound. In the midst of that frightening thunder and lightning and sounding of the trumpet, God spoke and the voice of the Lord was heard. The people were so terrified they were paralyzed with fear. They said to Moses, the man of God, "You go and talk to the Lord but don't let the Lord talk to us lest we die." So Moses went up on top of the mount and there received from God's hand the statutes and the judgments, the Book of the Covenant, the Book of the Law.

> And Moses came and told the people all the words of the LORD, and all the judgments: and all the people answered the one voice, and said, All the words which the LORD hath said will we do.
>
> And Moses wrote all the words of the LORD, and rose up early in the morning, and builded an altar under the hill, and twelve pillars, according to the twelve tribes of Israel.
>
> And he sent young men of the children of Israel, which offered burnt offerings, and sacrificed peace offerings of oxen unto the LORD.
>
> And Moses took half of the blood, and put it in basins; and half of the blood he sprinkled on the altar.

> And he took the book of the covenant, and read in the audience of the people: and they said, All that the LORD hath said will we do, and be obedient.
>
> And Moses took the blood, and sprinkled it on the people, and said, Behold the blood of the covenant which the LORD hath made with you concerning all these words." (Exod. 24:3-8).

One could not find in literature, in human experience, in drama, in fiction, or in history anything as impressive, as dramatic as the giving of the law. Evidently, it was something that God purposed and intended. It was not incidental. It was not an afterthought but rather it was central and dynamic in the purposes of God.

THE BREAKING OF THE LAW DID NOT SURPRISE GOD

Now, why did God give it? Was the Lord surprised that Israel and the whole human family break His law? Is that a new thing for God to learn about us, the children of old man Adam? Before the tables of stone could be taken down by Moses from the top of the mount and handed to the children of Israel, they were breaking that law. It was God Himself who said to Moses on the top of the mount, "Go, get thee down; for thy people, which thou broughtest out of the land of Egypt, have corrupted themselves" (Exod. 32:7). And when Moses took the two tables of the Ten Commandments written by the finger of God, incised in stone, and came down from the mount carrying those two tables, he heard the sound of laughter and merriment in the camp. When he drew nigh and could see, he looked upon a golden calf made by his brother Aaron. They were following a worship that the Israelites had learned in Egypt. A sacred bull or a sacred cow had become their god. Aaron, his own brother, had made a golden calf, and in keeping with the unspeakably carnal worship that they had learned in Egypt, the people had disrobed themselves and were dancing in an orgy around the calf, worshiping a sacred bull. When Moses looked upon it in volatile wrath and in anger, he took the tables of stone and broke them in pieces on a rock at the base of the mount. He lifted up his voice, and cried, "Who is on the LORD's side? let him come unto me" (Exod. 32:26).

That was no surprise to God that His commandments, His law, would be broken from the beginning. Why, then, the law?

No man has ever kept it. No man can keep it. No man will ever keep it, except the God-man Jesus Christ the Messiah, the promised seed of Abraham. There was no thought in God's mind that the people would be able to keep the law. No one has kept it but Christ. Because of that human weakness, four hundred thirty years before the law was given, God had made a way of salvation in mercy, in forgiveness, in love, in kindness, and in promise. God had done that four hundred thirty years before for Abraham and for the descendants of the patriarchal father.

But if all of that is true, Paul asks, "*Ti houn ho nomos?*" "Why the law?" Paul answers the question by stating two reasons. The law was added because of transgression; that is, it was given that we might see how fallen we are, "that sin might become exceeding sinful" (Rom. 7:13). No man can see his desperate need of God until first he realizes his own depraved and lost conditon. The world looks upon sin as a peccadillo, an incidental thing. It is just something that all of us somehow fall into. It is a little thing, it is inconsequential. To the unregenerated man it is the drag of our evolutionary ancestry and we are hardly accountable for it. That is the judgment of the world upon sin. But in God's sight, sin is a heinous aberration and we are personally responsible. Sin separates between us and God. It brings death to our bodies. We die because we are sinners. And it brings a second death, spiritual death, moral death to our souls. Thus the law was given that we might see how sinful we are, and how sinful sin is. The law is a plumbline that we might see how uneven is the wall of our lives. The law is an x-ray. It is a brilliant light to reveal the dark places hidden in our hearts. The law reveals to us how fallen and how depraved we are. Why the Law? It was added because of transgressions that we might see how sinful we are.

Second, Paul avows that the law was given in order that, being found sinners, all of us might be saved through faith in Jesus Christ. He is the seed of Abraham, the seed as of one; the promsed Deliverer who should be born of the patriarchal father. His coming is all important because we are so desperately and finally lost. Without that sense of needing to be saved, we have no sense of need for a Savior. The coming of Christ is peripheral, it is incidental, without that mighty purpose. Christ is not central, He is not all-meaningful, if we can be saved without Him. "If there had been a law given which could have given life, verily righteousness should have been by the law" (Gal. 3:21b). But because all of us fall short of the expectation of God, because all of us break the law, because all of us are sinful, we clearly see the heavenly office of the Savior. Being shown to be sinful by the perfect law, by the light of God, we are, therein, brought in our need, in our lostness, to Christ that we might be saved through mercy, grace, and atoning love in Him.

Our Desperate Need of a Savior

The man who is sick but has no sense of his illness would never seek out a physician. A man who is not in debt would never seek help to pay his debts. The man who is not incarcerated would never seek a pardon. It is the man who is incarcerated, who is in the penitentiary, who would seek a pardon. I wrote a letter to the Presdent of the United States recently asking for the pardon of a man whom I know. Had that man not been incarcerated, there would have been no need for the letter. It was because he was in the penitentiary that there was an appeal made for his pardon. When a man is well he does not seek a physician. It is because he is ill that he seeks the help of a doctor. If a man is not in debt there is no need to help him financially. But if a man is overwhelmed by indebtedness, he desperately needs help. Thus it is with us before God. We are debtors before God and cannot pay. We are dying and cannot find health and life. We are without hope in the world. We face nothing but corruption and after that the judgment of God. The purpose, therefore, of the law is to reveal to us our lostness, our sinfulness, our indebtedness, our fallen-shortness.

In that same law we are led to find mercy and forgiveness in Jesus our Lord. Without that sense of need, of lostness, we would never know the true and full meaning of Christ our Savior. There is no need for Christ if I can be saved by myself, in myself. As Paul wrote, "If there had been a law given which could have given life, verily righteousness should have been by the law" (Gal. 3:21b). There is no need for

Christ if a man can save himself. My impression, my experience, has been that when I talk to a man about the Lord and he begins to tell me how fine he is, there is nothing I can say, there is no Gospel to preach to him. When he says, "I am just, I am upright, I am righteous, I walk in decorum, in acceptability, and I live in integrity in my community and in the business world where I am"—when he says that all I can do is say: "That is so fine. Behold, a man of virtue, a man of intergity, a man of righteousness, a man of moral purity, a man of stature and acceptability, that is right!" But when a man, seeing God, hearing the voice of God, reading the law of God, finds himself a sinner lost, when he beats upon his breast, saying, "Lord, I am a lost man," then there is a Gospel message for him. It is only in his need, in his dying, in his lack, in his sin, in his shortcoming, in the confession of the weaknessess of his life that he comes to God and says, "Lord, have mercy upon me, a sinner." And that is the Gospel; namely, that God was in Christ, mediating to us in His atoning grace, in His forgiving mercy, all that God Himself could pour out upon us in love and forgiveness and salvation. But without that sense of need there is no meaningful Gospel to be preached to a lost man.

When I was a young fellow, I heard the then President of our Southwestern Seminary, Dr. Lee R. Scarbrough, preach in a revival meeting. He told the story of a little junior boy who came down the aisle in a service. The preacher described how he sat down by the little fellow and began to talk to him about his sin and about the Savior. When Dr. Scarbrough sat down with the little boy, the Sunday school teacher of the lad came down and sat on the other side. When he began to talk to the boy about being a sinner and about his need of the Savior, the Sunday school teacher broke in and said: "Dr. Scarbrough, excuse me, you are a stranger here, I know, and you are not acquainted with our people, but this little boy is the best boy in my Sunday school class and he is one of the finest boys in this community. You just do not understand." The preacher said that he ignored the Sunday school teacher and began to talk to the boy about sin, and about the need of the Savior. Then the teacher broke in again and said, "But

Dr. Scarbrough, I say you do not realize, this is a fine boy, the best boy in my class, and one of the finest I have ever known." Dr. Scarbrough said that he told the little boy, "You move over here." And he sat down between the Sunday school teacher and the little boy and then turning to the boy he said: "Son, do you realize that you are a sinner? Do you realize that you are lost? Do you realize you need a Savior?" And Dr. Scarbrough added that in just a few minutes, he led that boy into the kingdom of Christ. The lad found in Jesus the Savior for his soul, the one who could forgive his sins. Oh, that truth burned itself in my heart that day! There is no need for Christ if we can save ourselves. There is no need for Jesus if we can be righteous enough to walk with the redeemed into glory. It is because we are lost, it is because we are sinners that we must cast ourselves upon the grace and mercy of Christ, and without that lostness there is no Savior, nor is there any Gospel God can offer to us.

Often a little child, seeking to come down here to the front (let us say the child is four or five or six years old, just a little child), will say to the father and mother: "I want to go tell the pastor that I love Jesus. I love the Lord. I love Jesus." What I say to the father and mother always is: "Never interdict the child if the child says, 'Daddy, I want to go tell the pastor that I love Jesus.' Bring the little fellow down and we will pray." But on the card we record that decision as a "step toward God." Why is it not recorded as a conversion? The reason is that the child does not have a sense of sin. He does not have a sense of being lost. And without that sense of being lost, of being a sinner, Jesus cannot be a Savior. The child can love the Lord, he can love Jesus, but to be saved, to be regenerated, there has to come into his life that moment of accountability when the child sees, senses, feels that "I have done wrong, I am lost." Then it is that Christ can come in mercy and grace and open the door of salvation. By faith and by promise we enter in. He says, "Wherefore the law was the *paidagogos* (the tutor) to lead us to Jesus." The law was given to show us how far short we are, how desperately we need our blessed Lord. And it is a tutor, a *paidagogos,* to lead us to the mercy and grace that we know in Christ Jesus. And that is the Gospel—that He atoned for our sins, that He paid the penalty, that the judgment that should have fallen upon us fell upon Him, and that in His grace, in His stripes, in His suffering, we are healed.

Chapter 11

THE PAIDAGOGOS

Wherefore the law was our schoolmaster to bring us unto Christ, that we might be justified by faith. (Gal. 3:24)

The text of this chapter is Galatians 3:24 and the context will begin at verse 19: "Wherefore then serveth the law? It was added because of transgressions, till the seed should come to whom the promise was made; . . . Is the law then against the promises of God?" (vv. 3:19, 21a). Paul had previously said that four hundred thirty years before the law, Abraham and the seed of Abraham were saved by faith, by promise, by trusting the goodness and mercy of God. Four hundred thirty years after that proto-evangelium, God gave the law. The apostle, therefore, raises the question, why did God give it? In order to show what transgression really is, "that sin might become exceeding sinful." Then Paul asks, "Is the law then against the promises of God?" His answer is emphatic: "God forbid: for if there had been a law given which could have given life, verily righteousness should have been by the law. But the scripture hath concluded all under sin, that the promise by faith of Jesus Christ might be given to them that believe. But before faith came, we were kept under the law, shut up unto the faith which should afterwards be revealed. Wherefore the law was our *paidagogos* to bring us unto Christ, that we might be justified by faith. But after that faith is come, we are no longer under a *paidagogos*" (Gal. 3:21-25).

The Meaning and Office of the Paidagogos

Not in human experience, not in human life could there

have been chosen a more effective metaphor for an illustration of the law and the Gospel message than Paul used in choosing this word and symbol, *paidagogos*. The Greek word for "child" is *pais* and the genitive form of it is *paidos*. The Greek word for "lead" is *ago*. The Greek word for "leader" is *agogos*. Putting the two together, *paidos agogos, paidagogos,* we see the definition of the Greek word. It is "child leader."

In the days of the Graeco-Roman Empire slavery was most extensive. More than half of the population of the Roman Empire was chattel property. Had you walked down the streets of Ephesus, Corinth, or Antioch, in the lifetime of Paul, three of the five men you would have met on the street would have been slaves. They were owned by someone else. In those days noble and affluent Greek and Roman families placed their children in the care and keeping of a *paidagogos*. The assignment and responsibility of that slave was to watch over and to care for the youngsters. One of his assignments was to take the children and to deliver them to the *didaskalos,* the teacher. Thus Paul used that imagery of a *paidagogos,* taking the child by the hand and leading him in safety though in stern severity and discipline to the *didaskalos,* the teacher, to set forth the purpose of the law. He says that the law was our *paidagogos* (the child's tutor and leader) to deliver us to the Master Teacher, Christ, that we might be justified, that we might be saved, by His grace and mercy. For after faith has come, after we have been delivered to the teacher, there is no longer any need for the tutor, and we are no longer under the *paidagogos*. We are now in the hands of the Great Teacher.

We see from the passage and from the whole discussion in this letter to the churches of Galatia that it was never the intent of the law to save us. Rather, the purpose of the law was to reveal to us our need, our lack, our inability to commend ourselves in virtue and holiness to God, in order that we might be brought to Christ thus to be saved through His mercy, His promise, to be saved by grace and by trust.

The law was never intended to save us. It was not given for that purpose. The purpose of the law is to deliver us to Jesus, and after that office is filled and the purpose is achieved, there is no longer any need for the law. There is no law in heaven. There is no need for it. It has served its purpose, it is done. All of us in glory shall be like our Lord. We shall see Him as He is for we shall be like Him, so wrote the Apostle John (1 John 3:2). In heaven, therefore, the law-office is terminated. It has achieved the reason that it came into being, and its function is accomplished. We who are saved are forever under grace, under the loving mercy, goodness, and promises of God.

The Purpose of the Ceremonial and the Moral Law

Let us look at the law in two ways: first, the ceremonial law, and second, the moral law. The ceremonial law (the law of rites, rituals, and ceremonies, the offering on the altar, the spilling out of the blood, all of those things that go with the beautiful ritual of tabernacle and temple) was never in the purpose of God to save us. Rather, the purpose of the ceremonial law was to lead us to Jesus, to show us our Lord, to point the way to Him. They are pictures, symbols, types, and adumbrations of Him who is to come, the seed of Abraham. But it was never the purpose of God that these rituals, types, and symbols should ever be used to save us.

The ceremonial law, all of those things that pertain to the worship of the tabernacle and temple, was an instrument of God to point the way, but it is not the way itself. It is a map, it is not the country itself. It is a picture, it is not the thing itself. It is a presentation, it is not the substance itself. It is a portrait of the King, it is not the King himself. It is a picture of the banquet, it is not the feast itself. It is the shadow and type of things to come, it is not the reality and the substance itself. All the blood of all the sacrifices that were ever offered before God could never suffice to wash our sins away. It is not possible that the blood of bulls and of goats and the ashes of a heifer could be adequate or sufficient to wash the stain of sin out of our souls (Heb. 10:4, 9, 12, 13). As the author of the letter to the Hebrews points out, their ineffectiveness is demonstrated by the fact that they were repeated again and again. The sacrifices were offered over and over again. The reason for their continual offiering before God was they were able to save us, to deliver us from our sins. But the sacrifice of Christ, the atonement of Christ, the death of Christ, was once and for all. It is never repeated. Christ died once for our sins according to the Scripture, and that one atoning death is forever. It is all-adequate and all-sufficient. But the blood of bulls and goats poured out at the base of the altar could never save us, nor was it its intent to deliver us. It was a type, a picture that points us to Jesus. It is a *paidagogos* to take us to the Lord.

Let me speak of two of those pictures in the Old Testament. One is the Passover. All of the people in the land of Egypt are under the judgment of sin and of death. That night the death angel will visit the land. In every house there shall be mourning and lamentation because of death. But the Lord said that if a family would take a lamb, slay it, gather the blood in a basin and sprinkle it on the front of the house (on the lintel at the top and on the door posts on either side in the form of a cross), then when the angel of death visited the land that night, seeing the blood he would pass over that house and instead of death there would be life. There is no thought in the picture that the blood on the lintel and the door posts actually saves us, but it is a type, an adumbration, it is a *paidagogos* that leads us to the Lord Himself. This is what God did that He might teach us the meaning of the death of our Savior.

Another out of a multitude of those pictures in the ceremonial law is the manner of worship in the tabernacle and temple itself. The people were shut out of the presence of God (the Shekinah glory of God) by a thick, heavy veil. Just once a year could the high priest with blood of atonement go beyond that veil and there stand in the presence of the majesty of Jehovah. To come without blood would be immediate judgment and death. Is it not that the sprinkling of the blood saved the priest from the wrath and judgment of God, from the visitation of death, but it is a picture that shows us that in the death of Christ, in the blood of our Lord, we can stand in the presence of pure purity, of holy holiness, of sanctified sanctity and live. The whole ritual is a *paidagogos* to lead us to the atoning death and grace of our blessed Lord.

Now let me speak of the moral law. It was never the purpose of the moral law to save us, to deliver us from our sin.

We cannot exalt the moral law too highly. The moral law is like God Himself; it is perfect. It is a photograph of holiness. It is a picture of purity and perfection. It was written, it was inscribed into stone, by the very finger of God Himself, the Ten Commandments. No one can add to them nor can anyone take away from them. They are complete and perfect from the hand, mind, will, and purpose of God. Those Ten Commandments for western civilization are the foundation of all of our statutes and judgments.

If I am to be saved by the law, it is a simple way and a simple thing for me to do: keep that law and I shall be saved. The law says, "Do this and thou shalt have life." Nothing could be plainer than that. God wrote out His laws. Here are His commandments, His statutes, and His judgments. "Keep those statutes, obey those commandments, and thou shalt have life." But there is in it an addendum, and when I face that accompaniment I am thrown into abject, abysmal, and terrible despair. Though I keep ninety-nine of those statutes, if I fail in one, I am lost. Law observance is like a great chain. I do not have to break every one of those links to be crushed into the abyss that yawns beneath me. If I just break one link I fall. So it is written in the law, "Cursed (thus quoted Paul from Deuteronomy 27) is every one that continueth not in all things which are written in the book of the law to do them." Those horrible curses are written in the twenty-seventh and twenty-eighth chapters of the Book of Deuteronomy.

How Can a Man Under the Judgment of the Law Ever Be Saved?

What shall I do? This was the lament and the cry of the Apostle Paul in Romans 7. The law took occasion by the commandments and it slew me, it killed me. "What I would do (Paul wrote) I don't do, and what I don't do, that I would do. O wretched man that I am! Who shall deliver me from the body of this death?" For in law there is no place for repentance. There are no extenuating circumstances. There is no recognition of human fault and failure. The law is inexorable. It is impersonal. It is applied in justice, and "the soul that sins shall die," "the wages of sin is death." The moment

I sin I fall into the judgment and condemnation of the law. I am slain.

Do you remember how Bunyan's *Pilgrim's Progress* begins? It begins just like that—in despair, in lamentation and great crying. "As I walked through the wilderness of this world, I came upon a certain place where was a den, and I laid me down to sleep, and while I slept I dreamed a dream and behold a man standing with his back to his own house. He was dressed in rags. He was reading a Book, and there was a great burden on his back. As he read the Book, being no longer able to contain, he broke out with a great and lamentable cry saying, 'What shall I do?' I saw that he looked this way and that way as though he would run, but not knowing where to go he just stood still. Then while the Pilgrim cried and wept, Evangelist came up to him and said, "Why do you cry?" The man replied, "I read in this Book that it is appointed unto me to die, and after that the judgment. I'm not ready to do the first, and I'm not prepared to do the second. What shall I do to be saved?" And Evangelist replied, "Then ye must flee from the wrath to come." But the man replied: "But I don't know where to go. Whither shall I go and how shall I escape?" (That is the *paidagogos* to lead us to Jesus.) Evangelist said to the man: "Do you see yonder light? And just beyond the light the little wicker gate, and just beyond the wicker gate a hill and on the top of the hill a cross? There will you find the burden rolled away, and there will you find life and light and salvation." This is the purpose of the law, to condemn us, to show us our sins, to reveal ourselves and our lostness to ourselves, but not to lead us to despair, only to the despair of self. The purpose of the law is a *paidagogos* to lead us to Jesus that we might be saved by grace, by repentance, by promise, by His mercy. The law empties us that we might be filled with the fullness of God. The law strips us, it makes us bare and naked, that we might be clothed with the righteous garments of heaven. The law kills us, it slays us, it buries us, that we might be resurrected into the glory and life of Christ our Savior. The law is the *paidagogos* to lead us, to bring us, to deliver us to Jesus that we might be saved by faith, by trust, by grace, by the goodness and forgiveness and promise of God.

The Ways of Salvation Offered by the World

Now let me expatiate on that for a moment. The ways of evangelical salvation are so different from the ways of salvation offered by the world and by all other religions. Without exception, all other religions are filled with the hope of being saved by ourselves, by our good works. Without exception this is the attitude of the whole world, religious or non-religious, theistic or atheistic. We are saved by our good works. Talk to any man of any other religion, talk to any man anywhere in the world, and that is what he will tell you. He will extol himself, he will speak well of himself. He will say that he is not as vile as he could be, and I am sure that is true. It reminds me of the story of the town character who was as vile and wicked as old Satan himself. When he died there was no one to say anything good at his funeral. When they buried him the man at the cemetery said, "Isn't there anyone who will say something good about this man?" Eventually one fellow stood up, who had known him all his life, and said: "Yes, I can. He wasn't as bad all of the time as he was most of the time." Now, we have that attitude about ourselves. Most any man out in the world will commend himself. He is not as bad as that fellow over yonder, and he is not as vile as that other one, and he can remember when he could have done worse and he did better. So he will extol himself, he will defend himself, and he hopes to be saved, if there is such a thing as salvation, by his own merit, virtue, and goodness. He is going to be his own defender, his own savior, his own advocate, and his own mediator. He is going to take his chances by himself. He does not need Jesus and he does not need religion. He looks upon us Christians as people who need a crutch. He says: "I don't need a crutch when I walk through this world. And when I stand in the presence of God I will stand in my own merit without any help." That is the way of the world.

It would be wonderful if we could be saved like that. Paul admits, "If there had been a law given which could have given life, verily righteousness should have been by the law." (Gal. 3:21) In other words, it is a travesty, it is an unthinkable injustice that if a man can be saved by keeping a law, that Christ should have been delivered to death, to agony, to the suffering and dying of that awful crucifixion. But what is the Gospel? It is this, that no man is good enough to stand in the presence of God. The closer a man gets to the purity and the white light of the glory of God, the more it is evident that he is filled with sin. The very imaginations of his heart are evil all together. Finally in the presence of God he is blinded. No man can see the face of God and live. He is a sinful man and when he approaches the Almighty, the feeling and conviction of lostness, of sin, of unworthiness overwhelms him.

The sign of a man being a long way from God is his self-justification. "I will take my chances. I will stand on my own merit. I need no savior." A man who is far away is like that. But the man who draws nigh to God increasingly finds himself on his face, on his knees, crying for help, mercy, and forgiveness. That is the Gospel. The law revealing to us our sin is a *paidagogos* to bring us to Jesus. For the Gospel is this: you do not have to make payment for anything, it is already paid for you. All that is needed—the atonement, the suffering, the payment of sin—all of it is done for you. Christ Jesus has made salvation possible for me and all I do is just receive it. I just take it. There is nothing of me in my salvation. It is not the blood of Christ and then maybe my tears. It is not the good works of my Lord, and the merit of my Savior, and then some good works and merit of mine, too. No, it is all of Him. He paid it all, and what I do is receive it, I take it. And the issue of my salvation is not one of compatriotism with Jesus as though we are peers—He did some good and I did some good. No! What it is, is that our Lord did it all, and I just live in gratitude and in praise before Him. The issue of my life now is to thank Jesus. Oh, bless His name! What a glorious day when He washed my sins away! The Christian life is not one of working and grasping and striving and hoping. "Lord, maybe I can be good enough if I climb this ladder. If I climb and climb and climb maybe, finally, I'll find the top to lean against heaven." No, but the Christian life is, "O blessed Jesus, whose arms reached down and lifted me up out of the miry pit, and set my feet on the rock, and put a song in my heart, and the glory of God in my soul and I am on the road, Hallelujah! Praise His name! Glory, glory, glory!"

The purpose of the law, the apostle avows, is to reveal to us the "exceeding sinfulness of sin," because we have a tendency to look upon sin as a peccadillo. It is inconsequential, it is insignificant, it is a nothing. Do not think anything about it, forget it. That is our attitude toward sin. The puropse of the law is to point out to us how black, how dark, and how heinous sin is. He who could deliver us from a peccadillo is a nobody, but if sin is awesome and if judgment is terrible, then He who could save us from it is God Himself. Those two always go together: the tragedy of sin and the glory of the Savior who could deliver us from it.

The Purpose of the Tragic Illustrations in the Bible

An observaation was once made: "It seems to me that the God of the Old Testament was cruel. He is cruel in the extreme with Achan. After Jericho fell, because Achan took a wedge of silver and a wedge of gold and a beautiful Babylonish garment and hid it away, the Lord had him and all of his family stoned. And then when Elisha passed by and those children made fun of his bald head, bears came out of the woods at the command of the prophet and ate up forty-two of those children. Is not the God of the Old Testament cruel?" The answer is this: We have a tendency to extenuate. We have a tendency to excuse. We have a tendency to look upon sin as though it were a small thing—or nothing. But God looks upon sin as being dark, damnable, and heinous. Who would ever have thought that the sin of Adam and Eve would have plunged a whole world into destruction and all the generations have to endure the penalty of death. We do not realize the heinousness, the darkness, the judgment of God upon sin. And these things are written in the Bible for examples. Paul says so in I Corinthians 10:5, 6. These are examples that we might see the judgment of God upon wrong, upon our dereliction, upon our sin.

One time I mentioned the fact that sometimes we think how wonderful it would be to have been a member of that first-century church. It was filled with the Spirit of God and the power of the Lord upon it. And then you turn over the page and read where Ananias came and told a lie in the church, and he dropped dead. And then after awhile his wife, Sapphira, came in and told a lie, and she dropped dead. How would you like to belong to a church where all of the liars dropped dead? Why, the first Sunday one half of my church would be dead, and the next Sunday the other half would be dead! These things are in the Bible, written there for our admonition. They are examples. They show us how heinous and how dark is sin in our lives.

The law takes occasion by the commandment and it slays me; it reveals to me my real self. How dark is my life and how far short of the glory of God do I fall! The law is the *paidagogos* to take me to the Savior. Having revealed to me my lostness and my dereliction and my sin, the law is the *paidagogos* that leads me to Jesus who alone is the way of promise, of mercy, and of forgiveness to those who look in faith and acceptance, in repentance, in love, in trust to Him. God pours out upon the believer the spirit of adoption, and sonship, and forgiveness. "Welcome, son, welcome," says the Father to the prodigal boy. "Welcome, sweet lass, welcome, darling girl," says the Father to the sweet child who comes to Jesus in faith. God welcomes you, God welcomes me. That is what it is to believe in the Lord and that is what it is to become a Christian. "Lord, not in my works but in Thine. Not in my loveliness, but in Thine. Not in my merit, but in Thine. Not in my goodness, but in Thine. Lord, here I am, save me, take me, bless me, forgive me. Lord, do it now. Do it in the days of this pilgrimage. Do it in the hour of my death, and some day, O blessed Jesus, when we stand before the bema of Christ, stand by me, Lord, and see me thorugh." That is what it is to be a Christian.

Chapter 12

THE DOCTRINE OF JUSTIFICATION

"Wherefore the law was our schoolmaster to bring us unto Christ, that we might be justified by faith." (Gal. 3:24)

The Apostle Paul uses a word in the last verses of Galatians 3 that he has used several times heretofore. That word comprises the subject of this chapter, "Justification," or "Declared Righteousness." The Apostle writes: "Wherefore the law was our schoolmaster [our *paidagogos,* our tutor-leader, our child-leader,] to bring us unto Christ, that we might be justified by faith. But after that faith is come, we are no longer under a *paidagogos.* For ye are all the children of God by faith in Christ Jesus. For as many of you as have been baptized into Christ have put on Christ. There is neither Jew nor Greek, there is neither bond nor free, there is neither male nor female: for ye are all one in Christ Jesus. And if ye be Christ's, then are ye Abraham's seed, and heirs according to the promise" (Gal. 3:24-29).

That word "justified" is a word that Paul loves. In the second chapter, verse sixteen he says, "Knowing that a man is not justified by the works of the law, but by the faith of Jesus Christ, even we have believed in Jesus Christ, that we might be justified by the faith of Christ, and not by the works of the law: for by the works of the law shall no flesh be justified." Then he uses the same word (except it will be translated differently) in Galatians 3:6, "Even as Abraham believed God, and it was accounted to him for justification" (here the word is translated "righteousness"). In 3:11 the apostle writes, "But that no man is justified by the law in the sight of God, it is evident: for, The just shall live by faith."

Righteousness and Justification Are the Same Words

It is interesting that in both Hebrew and in Greek, in the Old Testament and in the New Testament, the same root words are translated "righteousness" and "justification." The Hebrew word for righteousness is *tsedeq.* It is also defined "to be declared righteous," "to be righteous," or "to be justified." In Genesis 15:6, which is quoted in Galatians 3:6, "Abraham believed God and his faith was counted for *tsedaqah,* righteousness, justification."

The Greek word *dikaios* can be translated "just" or "righteous." In Matthew 1:19 we are told that when Joseph saw that Mary was already with child, he being a *dikaios* man (a "just" man), sought to put her away privately. In Matthew 5:45, God sendeth the rain on the *dikaios* and the *adikos,* the "just" and the "unjust." In Matthew 9:13 the Lord says He came not to call the *dikaios,* the "righteous," but "sinners" to repentance. The words are the same for "righteous" and 'just." In Acts 10:22, Cornelius the centurion is described as a *dikaios* man, translated there a "just" man. In Romans 1:17, the text says "The just (the *dikaios*) shall live by faith." In Romans 3:10 the Scripture avows that "there is none righteous *(dikaios),* no, not one." It is the same word.

The verbal form of *dikaios,* "just," "righteous," is *dikaioo,* which means "to pronounce or treat as righteous," "to hold guiltless," "to justify." For example, in Luke 18:14 there is the story of the publican who would not lift up his eyes to heaven but rather beat on his breast, saying, "Lord, be merciful to me, a sinner." Jesus says he went down to his home *dikaioo,* "justified, declared righteous, guiltless." In Romans 6:30 Paul says whom God called He *dikaioo,* He "justified": and whom He *dikaioo,* whom He "justified," He also glorified.

Now there is another word that is built upon that root, *dikaios,* meaning "just," "righteous." It is *dikaiosis* which means "acquittal," "justification." If a man was tried before a bar, before a court, and he was acquitted, this is the word that one would use to describe it: *dikaiosis.* He was "acquitted," he was "justified." In Romans 4:25 that word is used: Christ was delivered for our offenses, and He was raised again for our "acquittal," for our "justification." Paul uses that word again in Romans 5:18, "Therefore as by the offence of one judgment came upon all men to condemnation; even so by the righteousness of one the free gift came upon all men unto justification *(dikaiosis)* of life." So the word "righteous" and "justification" mean the same thing. "To declare righteous" is the meaning of "to justify," "to be acquitted," "to be held guiltless."

Justification, then, is that judicial act whereby God for Jesus' sake looks upon us as being blameless, without sin, without spot. In His sight we have been made to be holy and pure. Justification is something that God does, looking upon us who are actual sinners. He justifies us, He declares us righteous, He grants us acquittal. We are not under condemnation. God does this on account of the atonement of Christ. We are joined to our Lord by faith, we are baptized into Christ, we are made a part of His body in our acceptance of Him, and as such God justifies us, He declares us righteous. He acquits us of all of the penalty and condemnation upon our sins and transgressions.

The Remarkable Bible Doctrine of Justification

This is one of the most remarkable doctrines that one will find in the Bible. The teaching is not a new thing, as though it were first brought to us in the pages of the New Testament. Rather, it is God's way of looking upon His people. He looks upon us ideally, even though we are not ideal. We are not spotless, we are not sinless, yet God looks upon us, loves us, as though we were. Look at this, for example, in Numbers 23. Balak, the king of Moab, has hired Balaam (a prophet) to curse Israel. But when Balaam took up his parable to curse Israel, he blessed Israel instead: "And he took up his parable, and said, Balak the king of Moab hath brought me from Aram, out of the mountains of the east, saying, Come, curse me Jacob, and come, defy Israel. How shall I curse, whom God hath not cursed? or how shall I defy, whom the Lord hath not defied? And Balak said unto Balaam, What hast thou done unto me? I took thee to curse mine enemies, and, behold, thou hast blessed them altogether" (vv. 7, 8, 11). And in the prophecy Balaam replies to Balak, "He hath not beheld iniquity in Jacob, neither hath he seen perverseness in Israel" (v. 21). What an amazing statement! When one reads the story of the children of Israel in the wilderness, he will find it to be a story of perverseness, of stubbornness, of stiff-neckedness, of unbelief. And yet the Scriptures will say that God "hath not beheld iniquity in Jacob, neither hath he seen perverseness in Israel." Well, what is that? It is that glorious, incomparably, immeasurably dear and precious attitude of God toward His people. In His sight we can do no wrong. We are justified, we are declared righteous, as God looks upon His children.

Let us take another illustration. This one will be taken from the prophet Zechariah. "And [the Lord] shewed me Joshua the high priest (Zerubbabel was the civic leader and Joshua, the high priest, was ecclesiastical leader in the return of the exiles to Jerusalem from the Babylonian captivity) standing before the angel of the LORD, and Satan standing at his right hand to resist him" (3:1). Joshua the high priest, as he stood before God, had at his right hand Satan standing to condemn him, to abuse him, to resist him. Why? Because Joshua was clothed in filthy garments. The high priest, clothed with sin, his garments unrighteous, gave opportunity for Satan to accuse him, saying: "Look at him. Look at his filthy rags. Look at his unkempt life. Look at the sin in his heart. The very imaginations of his soul are evil altogether." Satan had cause to condemn the priest, for Joshua was clothed with filthy garments.

But the story does not end there. There is more, much more. Let us continue to read. "And the LORD said unto Satan, The LORD rebuke thee, O Satan; even the LORD that hath chosen Jerusalem rebuke thee: is not this a brand plucked out of the fire?" (v. 2). He is a soul that I have saved, "And unto him he said, Behold, I have caused thine iniquity to pass from thee, and I will clothe thee with a change of raiment. And I said, let them set a fair mitre [a beautiful head piece] upon his head. So they set a fair mitre upon his head, and clothed him with garments" (vv. 4b, 5). The high priest then appeared with his beautiful raiment. There is that doctrine of justification again. Was Joshua clean? No. Was he faultless? No. Was he sinless? No. Was he filled with imperfections? Yes. Was he clothed with filthy garments? Yes. When Satan stood at his right hand to condemn him, he had cause to do so, for Joshua was a sinner man. But the Lord said to Satan, "The Lord rebuke thee, for I have saved him, and he is mine; he is a brand plucked out of the burning." And the Lord further said, "Take away his filthy garments and place upon him the beautiful garments of heaven. Set a mitre upon his head, for I have chosen him." Not that Joshua was righteous, but God declared him righteous. Thus the Lord looked upon him beautifully, ideally, gloriously, as one justified in the sight of God.

"Moerover whom he did predestinate, them he also called: and whom he called, them he also justified" (Rom. 8:30). Justification is something God does for us. "And whom he justified, them he also glorified." "Who shall lay anything to the charge of God's elect?" It is God that justifies us. Who shall say anything about God's people? Who shall condemn them in heaven, in earth, or under the earth in the lower world, in another world? The Lord looks upon us and declares us righteous, and in His sight we are. The Lord accepts all of us who are identified with Christ as He accepts His own Son. Justification is an idealization by which God accepts us as perfect, sinless.

An agriculturalist will look at a little twig bursting out of the ground and, being knowledgeable, he will say, "That is an oak." An oak? To me an oak is a vast, spreading tree with branches and leaves, a tremendous creation. An oak has acorns, and it can withstand the most terrible of winds and storms. That is an oak. But the agriculturalist will look at that little twig and he says that it is an oak. What he is doing is this: he is idealizing, for all of the possibilities of the great tree are in that tiny twig. Its incipient development is a harbinger of what is yet to come, and he looks upon it in the knowledge of ideally what it can and will be. So God looks upon us. We are so tiny and so small and so weak. Most any little thing can just blow us over. But God looks upon us ideally—what we are going to be in Christ, in glory—and that is justification. He declares us righteous.

The Judgment of the World in Contrast With the Judgment of God

Let me speak of this heavenly justification by way of contrast in order that it might be the more vividly impressed upon our hearts. The way the world judges men is by their works. People accept the person according to his works. Any sensible man in the world would defend that. The criterion is very logical and most reasonable. Rulers and leaders judge, they accept, they promote, they demote the man according to his works. But God does just the opposite. First, God looks at the man, then God looks at his works. In God's sight it is always first the man. He accepts the person of the man, what he is, what he is in his heart, then God will look at the man's work. Let me show that to you in the story of Cain and Abel. The story says, "And in process of time it came to pass, that Cain brought of the fruit of the ground an offering unto the LORD. And Abel, he also brought of the firstlings of his flock and of the fat thereof. And the LORD had respect unto Abel and to his offering: But unto Cain and to his offering he had not respect. And Cain was very wroth, and his countenance fell" (Gen. 4:3-5). First, God accepted Abel, the man himself, then He accepted his offering. But God rejected Cain first, then He rejected Cain's offering. God accepts or rejects the person of a man first, then He accepts or rejects the man's works. But always first it is God's respect and acceptance of the man himself.

One will find that judgment of the Lord clearly followed in the Bible. Look at the twenty-third Psalm: "The LORD is my shepherd; I shall not want. He maketh me to lie down in green pastures: he leadeth me beside the still waters. He restoreth my soul: he leadeth me in the paths of righteousness for his name's sake." First, God looks at the man's heart. He accepts the man himself, and then he accepts or rejects the man's works.

I think of Samuel who was sent to the house of Jesse to anoint the new king over Israel. This Jesse had all seven of his sons pass before Samuel. The eldest was Eliab who was tall, strong, and handsome. When Samuel saw him walk before him, he said, "Surely, surely the Lord's anointed is standing here before me, a fine specimen of a man." But the Lord said, "I have rejected him." Then Jesse had Abinadab, his second son, pass before the prophet. As Samuel looked upon him, strong and magnificent, he said, "Surely, the Lord's anointed stands before me." But the Lord said, "I have rejected him." Then Jesse had his third son, Shammah, stand before the prophet.

But the Lord said, "I have refused him, also." Then Samuel said: "Master, I do not understand. I never saw such fine looking young men." The Lord answered, "Samuel, your trouble is that you look on the outside, but God looks on the heart." All seven of those boys passed by, and the Lord said, "I have rejected them all." In despair Samuel turned to Jesse and said: "Are these all of your boys? I do not understand. God sent me here to the house of Jesse to anoint a king for Israel, and you have had all seven of your sons pass by in front of me. Do you have another boy?" And Jesse said: "You know, I forgot about him. I have a little boy who is keeping the sheep. He is out there with his harp singing songs to the sheep." Samuel said, "We will not sit down until you fetch him." They brought in that boy. The Scriptures describe him as being ruddy, fair-haired, unshaven. God said immediately to Samuel, "This is he; arise, anoint him!" (cf. 1 Samuel 16:5-12) God accepts first the man, then he accepts the man's works.

The Real Man Is Revealed in His Heart

Now let me illustrate that doctrine in human life. In the days of the depression as a youth I was in Chicago. I happened to be with a young fellow from Seattle, the son of a rich man who sent the boy away to get rid of him (his step-mother did not want him around). He was the most knowledgeable, worldly young fellow I was ever with. For one thing, he knew all about Al Capone. I wondered as a youngster how Al Capone could hold the city of Chicago in the palm of his hand. How? Well, I went around with the young fellow and I soon found out. He took me to one Al Capone's speak-easies, right in the middle of town at Madison and State Streets, under the nose of forty policemen who patrolled up and down there every day. I looked at their illegal gambling and their illegal drinking. It was an astonishment to me, the number of those speak-easies all over the city. Then that young fellow and I looked at Al Capone's operation. The Lord only knows how many thousands, and, I suppose, millions of dollars that Al Capone poured into feeding the poor and taking care of the widows and the orphans. He had every precinct bound up in the hollow of his hand. When time came to vote for aldermen, and time came to vote for mayor, all of those people followed the slate of

Al Capone to the tee and the law could not touch him. The people who were starving to death, when they received food and coal from Al Capone, were overwhelmed by the goodness and the generosity of the man. Was Capone actually a worthy man? He was a gangster and a murderer of the vilest sort. Not only God, but the law-abiding citizens of the United States looked at Al Capone and said that he was a leech, a curse. Yet they were unable to touch him because of his good works. They finally sent him to the penitentiary because of his income tax returns. This is an illustration of how men look and how God looks at man's deeds.

We seek to commend ourselves to God. The world seeks to commend itself to God by its good works. "Look at me, Lord. Look at me." But God says our good works are like filthy rags in His sight, and if we are ever to be justified we must be justified by faith in Christ. For by the works of the law, by doing good deeds shall no man be declared righteous. If we are ever accepted in the eyes of God, it must be in His grace and favor through Christ our Lord. There is no other way. And that is the Bible doctrine of justification. It is a declared righteousness, it is an imputed righteousness. It is something God does for us, when we take our poor lost souls to Jesus.

As Paul begins Galatians 4, he contrasts the man who seeks salvation by good works with the man who comes to God by faith. Paul describes the two in the parable, in the similitude, of a slave in the house and the son of the owner. He says that the slave in the house is a slave forever working, a workman, but the child is the heir. When the child comes of age, God gives to him all of the inheritance of the estate. Now let me say that in my words. When a man tries to save himself by his good works, the more he works, the more he is in debt because not any of his works are perfect. So he gets behind, and behind, and behind, and the more work he does the more it is a debt, a debt, a debt, because his works always have in them the element of imperfection. No man is able to do anything perfectly. He cannot even pray perfectly, nor can he believe perfectly. He has to cast himself upon the mercies of God. So the reward of works is debt, and debt, and more debt, and more debt. So it is with the slave. The servant who works in the house just works there forever and he is still a slave. At the end of his lifetime, having worked a lifetime in the house, he is still a hired servant. But the son, the child—ah, the father looks upon him as his own flesh and kin and blood, and he becomes the heir of all of his father's estate.

The vital difference between a servant who works and a son who is a child of the father is found in the parable, in the story of the prodigal son. The boy came back and said to his father, "Father, I have sinned against heaven and before thee, and am no more worthy to be called thy son: make me as one of thy hired servants" (Luke 15:18b, 19). Just put me to work and let me show you by my works that I have repented and that I want to come back home and that I want to be in my father's house. Make me a hired servant. Did the father say: "That is a wonderful idea, son. You come here and work in this house and on the farm like a hired servant, and at the end of five years or ten years or twenty years, or a lifetime, after I have watched you work and you have demonstrated your work, then I will look upon you and consider taking you back into the family and into the household"? Is that what the father said? When the boy said, "Dad, I have sinned and I am no more worthy to be called thy son, make me as one of thy hired servants"—when the boy started off with his speech the father broke in and said: "Bring hither the finest robe; put it upon him. Take off those old rags. Bring hither the ring of inheritance, the sign of his dignity, and put it on his hand. Put shoes on his feet, for this my what? This my *son!* This *my son* was dead, and is alive again. He was lost and is found." That is justification. We do not work for it. We are not slaves. Justification is of grace, it is of love, it is of God's favor and goodness. When He receives us as a child, as a son, all of the goodnesses of Christ and all of the righteousnesses of heaven are ours. They belong to us. They are imputed to us. They are given to us and we are declared righteous in His presence.

So many times, reading that Book, trying to understand what God has done for us in Christ, I am overwhelmed! Ah, the greatness and goodness of God that reaches even to us who are so frail and so sinful and so lost!

Chapter 13

THE FULLNESS OF TIME

> But when the fulness of the time was come, God sent forth his Son, made of a woman, made under the law. (Gal.4:4)

Four Greeks words in the text immediately command our attention. They are: *To pleroma tou kronou.* They mean literally "when the full number of days had arrived, when full preparation was made." At that end of the time of preperation God sent forth His Son, made of a woman, born of a virgin, made under the law to be the Savior of the world.

As I ponder the text, immediately there floods into my mind the story of the preparation of God in history for the birth of His Son. "When the fulness of the time was come, God sent forth his Son, made of a woman." God moves, God acts in time, in ages, and in centuries. The Lord works unhurriedly, without haste. Sometimes it is aeons and aeons before God brings to pass that holy purpose that He has in His heart, but He never changes. He works and in His sovereign will and grace these great movements progress forward under His surveillance.

Think of the ages that God took in the formation of this planet. Have you been to the Grand Canyon? At the top will be a geological stratum and beneath that another, and beneath that another, and beneath that another, and another, and another, and down, and down goes the record of God's work through the aeons and the ages. God's timelessness is written there in the rocks. Looking a mile down, one gazes on the course of the Colorado River in its serpentive, circuitous, tortorous path through solid, basalt, black rock. Geologists who date the course of the ages will say that that black, basalt rock in the bottom, buried beneath the strata above, at one time were mountains twenty-six thousand feet high but the ages wore them away, and finally other ages buried them in the record that is seen in that yawning abyss of the Grand Canyon.

So it is with mankind. God works in human history. To us the age of man seems so elongated, but the geologists say that if one were to compare the age of the earth to the age of man it would be like comparing the height of the Empire State Building (one thousand two hundred fifty feet) with the thickness of a nickel (barely one-eighth of an inch). Yet always the sovereign grace of God does move. Thus it is here: "When the fulness of the time was come." God moved through the centuries and brought to pass this epochal moment.

To pleroma, "the full days," *tou kronou,* "the exact time." Theer was an exact time, known to God, chosen of the Lord, when the Christ should be born. There was an exact time when He should die. There was an exact time when He should be raised from the dead. There was an exact time when He should ascend into heaven. There is an exact time, known but to Him, when the Lord shall descend in glory from above. The power, the sovereign grace of God moves in human history. "When the fulness of the time was come, God sent forth his Son, made of a woman, made under the law" (a member of the household of the Jewish race and faith).

The Religious Preparation for the Coming of Christ

Let us look at four moving purposes of God as the Lord shaped the whole civilized world for the coming of that birth in Bethlehem. First, is the religious preparation. As I think of the hand of God among the Jewish people, preparing for the coming of the Savior of the world, I think first and foremost of the Babylonian captivity. There could have been no sorrow like the sorrow of those forlorn and displaced people when they saw their temple destroyed, their holy city go up in flame and fire, destroyed by the fury of the Babylonian armies, and finally looked upon their people carried into captivity (Lam. 1:12). To them it was the disaster of all disasters. One can feel somewhat the sense of the tragic sorrow of those enslaved, up-rooted people in the one hundred thirty-seventh Psalm:

> "By the rivers of Babylon, there we sat down, yea, we wept, when we remembered Zion.
>
> We hanged our harps upon the willows in the midst thereof.
>
> For there they that carried us away captive required of us a song; and they that wasted us required of us mirth, saying, Sing us one of the songs of Zion.
>
> How shall we sing the LORD's song in a strange land?
>
> If I forget thee, O Jerusalem, let my right hand forget her cunning.
>
> If I do not remember thee, let my tongue cleave to the roof of my mouth; if I prefer not Jerusalem above my chief joy." (vv. 1-6).

Oh, the sadness of the tragedy of the Babylonian captivity! Yet out of it came three monumental events, each one of which prepared for the coming of Christ.

One, the Jewish people were thereafter and forevermore monotheistic. They were never idolatrous again. The Persians, being Zoroastrians, were monotheists. As such, they were in deepest sympathy with the Jews. Under Persian guidance the children of Abraham were given opportunity to return home. The Magi were Zoroastrian priests. They came a vast distance from the East to bow down before the newborn King. Out of the Babylonian captivity the Jews were forever and thereafter monotheists.

Second, out of that Babylonian captivity came the Canon of the Holy Scriptures. Under Ezra and the following members of the Great Synagogue, the holy writings inspired of God were gathered together and were taught to the people and reverenced by the nation.

And third, out of the Babylonian catpivity came the institution of the synagogue. It is that kind of a service and that type of a gathering together that we enjoy as the church of Jesus Christ today. All over the civilized world were those synagogues organized, and in them were the Holy Scriptures taught. From these Scriptures and from these synagogue services there was created a world expectancy that out of the East there should come a Savior and a Deliverer for all mankind. How little did the Jewish people realize that in the tears and sobs and sorrow of the loss of their homeland and their deportation to the Mesopotamian Valley, the sovereign hand and purpose of God was preparing for the coming of the Savior into the world!

Out of the tragedy and out of sorrow come practically all of the blessings of God in human life. I think of the first Christian martyr. When Stephen was stoned to death, the Scriptures say that devout men buried him and made great lamentation over him. Yet look at the next sentence. Upon the persecution that arose around Stephen, the disciples were scattered everywhere preaching the Word. Look at the next chapter which begins with the words, "And Saul was consenting unto his death." When Saul of Tarsus saw the martyrdom of Stephen, the faithfulness of the deacon stayed in his mind and in his soul. (This is the meaning of Acts 9:5, "It is hard for thee to kick against the pricks.") Through the suffering of Stephen God changed the persecuting Saul of Tarsus into the flaming evangelist and missionary Paul. The apostle was born in the death and in the martyrdom of Stephen.

The Cultural Preparation for the Birth of Christ

We turn now to the cultural preparation for the birth of Christ. In about 350 B.C. there arose in Macedon a mighty military conqueror named Alexander, the Son of the Macedonian King, Phillip. In the heart of Alexander was the ambition to conquer the world. This thing he did in a comparatively short span of twelve years. When Alexander the Great moved his army to overwhelm the nations of the East, he carried with him his teacher, Aristotle, the philosopher. So significant and so permanent was the influence of the conquest of Alexander that the entire world became Greek. The world became Greek in its culture, in its philosophy, in its institutions, in its art, in its drama, in its literature, in its architecture, in its thought, in its patterns of life, and in its language. Little did Alexander the Great know that he was preparing for the preaching of the Gospel of Christ to all men everywhere.

Alexander was followed by his four generals who divided the Alexandrian empire into four quadrants. They continued that Greek life and culture. In Egypt in 280 B.C. the Holy Scriptures of the Hebrews were translated into Greek, called the Septuagint. That version was the Bible that the first apostles and disciples of Christ used for the preaching of the Gospel to the Mediterranean world. When Paul wrote his letter to the church at Rome he wrote it in Greek. When John, the sainted disciple, beloved of the Lord, wrote the Savior's seven letters to the churches of Asia in the Apocalypse, he wrote them in Greek. The language was the universal nomenclature of distinction, of culture, and of intellectual teaching. Little did Alexander the Great realize that he was in the hand and purpose of God in his conquest of the civilized world. "When the fulness of the time was come, God sent forth his son, made of a woman."

The Political Preparation for the Birth of Christ

We discuss now the political preparation God made for the coming of Christ. In the peninsula that on a map looks to us like a boot in the heart of the Mediterranean, there was a little city called Roma. It was the capital of a small province. Despite their small country, the Romans themselves were powerful. They were disciplined, they were fierce, and they were mighty warriors. That little province controlled finally all the countries around it and eventually conquered the entire peninsula. The Romans spilled over into Europe above and then into Africa below and finally into the Middle East beyond. They had a genius for government and for pulling differing peoples together. They laced the entire civilized world with paved Roman roads which are traveled on today. One could easily go from one side of the empire to the other. Travelers and merchants could go from one end of the Mediterranean to the other without fear of molestation. The Romans destroyed the pirates on the sea and the robbers on the land. The Romans inaugurated the finest postal system that the earth had ever known so that letters could be written and carried in dispatch all over the known world.

The Romans created the Pax Romana, "the universal peace." The shrine of their god, Janus (who has two faces, looking this way, looking that way, the god of doors and gateways) in Rome was closed when there was peace. The month of January is named for him. The doors to the shrine of Janus were closed when Christ was born. There was universal peace and men could go everywhere preaching, teaching, proclaiming, announcing the good news of the birth of the Son of God.

Little did the Romans realize that in creating their empire they were preparing the earth for the coming of the Christ. The Scriptures say in the first chapter of Luke that when God sent Gabriel from heaven to announce to a virgin Jewess that she should be the mother of this foretold, foreordained child, He sent the angel to a little city in Galilee named Nazareth. But Micah, seven hundred years before, had said that the babe would be born in Bethlehem in Judaea. "And there went out a decree from Caesar Augustus that all the earth should be enrolled" (a census, possibly for tax purposes). And according to the custom of the Jewish people, Joseph of Nazareth went up to Bethlehem there to be enrolled with Mary, his espoused wife, being great with child, for they were of the lineage and household of David. And while she was there the fullness of the time came, when God sent forth his Son, born of a virgin, made of a woman. This is the hand of God in human history. Little did Caesar Augustus realize that when he made that decree he was carrying out the infinite, sovereign purposes of the Almighty.

The Personal Preparation for the Birth of Christ

We look now at the personal preparation for the birth of the Messiah. Sometimes it is impossible for us to enter into the infinitude of the mind of God. For example, the Scriptures say that Christ was the lamb slain from before the foundation of the earth. Before God flung these stars into space and spoke the planets into orbit, He planned the gift of His Son and provided for His sacrificial death. The way of salvation for our lost souls was in the heart of God before the earth was made, before the foundations were laid. The Almighty purposes to send His Son to be one of us in order that He might be our friend and personal Savior. Thus it behooved Him not to take upon Him the form of angels, but He took upon Him the seed of Abraham and He was made like unto us that He might be a faithful high priest, understanding, sympathetic, merciful. In heaven he volunteered to be our brother and our sacrifice for sin.

God worked out that purpose of incarnation through the

centuries and the generations in the earth. In the third chapter of the Book of Genesis the Lord said the Messiah will be born of a woman. The seed of the woman shall crush Satan's head. In Genesis 12 (and thereafter) the Messiah is to be the seed of Abraham, "for in thy seed, as of one, shall all of the families of the earth be blessed." In Genesis 49 we learn that the prophet Jacob (turning to his fourth son, Judah) said, "The sceptre shall not depart from Judah, nor a lawgiver from between his feet, until Shiloh come." The Savior will be born of the tribe of Judah. In 2 Samuel 7 we learn that God promised to David a son who shall sit upon his throne and reign forever and ever, "and of his kingdom there shall never be an end." In Micah 5 we read the coming King is to be born in the little city of David called Bethlehem.

Upon a day of days and upon a night of nights, "when the fulness of the time was come God sent forth his Son, made of a woman, made under the law." According to the mandate of government Joseph, with his espoused wife, Mary, being great with child, made their way to Bethlehem. And in that night, in the fullness of the time, when the exact moment came for which God had moved in all the ages and in all history, the child was born. The heavens opened and the angels who had been in expectancy, watching the sovereign God through those ages, the angels in their hopes came down, and to the startled, watching shepherds announced: "For unto you is born this day in the city of David a Saviour, which is Christ the Lord. And this shall be the sign unto you; ye shall find the babe wrapped in swaddling clothes, (just rags around Him), lying in a manger" (Luke 2:11, 12). And the shepherds were invited to go and see for themselves. Then, unable to contain heaven's joy any longer (the moment of moments had come), the angels burst into song, "Glory to God in the highest and on earth peace, good will toward men." "In the fulness of the time, God sent forth his Son, made of a woman, made under the law."

There's a song in the air!
There's a star in the sky!
There's a mother's deep prayer
And a baby's low cry!

There's a tumult of joy
O'er the wonderful birth,
For the Virgin's sweet boy
Is the Lord of the earth.

And the star rains its fire
while the beautiful sing,
For the manger of Bethlehem
cradles a King!

Ay! the star rains its fire
while the beautiful sing,
For the manger of Bethlehem
cradles a King!

"When the fulness of the time was come, God sent forth his Son, made of a woman, made under the law," to redeem us from the curse of the law that we might receive the adoption of sonship, whereby we cry, Abba, Father. The God of time, the God of the centuries, the God of history, the God of all the ages, the God of the present, the God of the future, the God of glory, is the God whom some day we shall see face to face, even Jesus Christ.

Chapter 14

THE DOCTRINE OF ADOPTION

> But when the fulness of the time was come, God sent forth his Son, made of a woman, made under the law,
> To redeem them that were under the law, that we might receive the adoption of sons. (Gal. 4:4, 5)

In Galatians 4:1 and following Paul writes: "Now I say, That the heir, as long as he is a child, differeth nothing from a servant, though he be lord of all; But is under tutors and governors until the time appointed of the father. Even so we, when we were children, were in bondage under the elemnts of the world: But when the fulness of the time was come, God sent forth his Son, made of a woman, made under the law, To redeem them that were under the law, that we might receive the adoption of sons. And because ye are sons, God hath sent forth the Spirit of his Son into your hearts, crying, Abba, Father. Wherefore thou art no more a servant (a *doulos,* a slave), but a son (a *huios*); and if a son, then an heir of God through Christ" (vv. 1-7). Or as Paul wrote in Romans 8, one becomes a joint-heir with Christ of all of God's riches in glory.

The True and Triune God

When I look at this passage I see that Paul has written into it the name of the triune God, the Trinity of our experience in God: God the Father, God the Son, and God the Holy Spirit. God the Father sent forth His Son and also the Spirit of His Son, the Holy Spirit. These three are one, the one God who in experience we know as three. To bow before each one and to pray to each one is to pray to God and to worship before God.

If I were to bow and pray to Abraham Lincoln, I would feel uneasy doing it and so would you. If I bowed in prayer and addressed my supplication to Mahavira, to Krishna, to Buddha, to Confucius, I would feel like an idolator and you would also. But if I bow on my knees and pray to God the Father, or pray to God the Son, or pray to God the Holy Spirit, I feel in my soul a perfect quietness and congruity, and so do you. For we know God in experience and in life as triune. We know Him as Father, we know Him as Savior, and we know Him incarnate in our hearts, the living, indwelling Spirit of God.

It is God who has begotten us again to a living hope by the resurrection of Jesus Christ from the dead. It is God our Savior who has redeemed us from our sins by His own precious blood. And it is God the Holy Spirit who has quickened us, regenerated us, and received us into the kingdom of the Father. It is the Holy Spirit who has given us the seal of the assurance of our salvation by His presence in our souls, who is omnipresent, who is incarnate in the believer and in His church. If I pray to each one, I have a perfect feeling of fitness, of appropriateness, and you do, too.

The one true God is God our Father whom we know as our heavenly Father, God our Savior whom we know as our Savior, and God the Holy Spirit who dwells in our hearts. They lead us to the deep, precious and wonderful things of Christ who reveals the Lord to us in all His glory and beauty, His meaning and significance. This is the doctrine of the Trinity that Paul has enwoven into this passage in the fourth chapter of the Book of Galatians.

There is no finer doxolgy than "Gloria Patri":

> Glory be to the Father, and to the Son,
> and to the Holy Ghost;
> As it was in the beginning, is now,
> and ever shall be, world without end. Amen.

That is the Christian faith.

"When the fulness of the time was come, God sent forth his Son, made of a woman, made unto the law, to redeem them that were under the law, that we might receive the adoption of sons. And because ye are sons, God hath sent forth the Spirit of his Son into your hearts, crying, Abba, Father" (Gal. 4:4-6).

Paul's Use of the Word "Adoption"

The Greek word *huiothesia,* translated "adoption," is peculiar to Paul. He uses it several times in the New Testament. It is made up of *thesia,* "placing," and *huios,* "son." Putting them together it means "placing a son," putting him in the family. For you see, by nature we are not children of God. There is no such thing as the doctrine of the universal fatherhood of God and the universal brotherhood of man, not in the Bible. God is the great creator, the Father of all mankind, but by nature, by birth, we are sinful people and sin shuts us out, separates us from God. As Paul says in Ephesians 2:1, "And you hath he quickened, who were dead in trespasses and sins." Not only has the Holy Spirit quickened us, regenerated us, given us a new birth (and that not by the will of man, nor by the will of the flesh), but also in this new birth, in that regeneration, we are adopted into the family of God.

Three times in the Old Testament was there an actual adoption. Moses was the adopted son of Pharaoh in Egypt. In 1 Kings 11, Genubath, the son of Hadad, was adopted into the family of the reigning monarch of the Nile. And in Esther 2 we are told that Esther was the adopted daughter of Mordecai, her uncle.

The Incomparable Privileges of the Adopted Children of God

There is an adoption for all of us who have come to know God in Christ, and as such we have incomparable privileges. They are the privileges of a son. Paul names several of these endowments. The first one is, "Wherefore thou art no more a *doulos* (a slave), but a *huios* (son); and if a son, then an heir of God through Christ" (Gal. 4:7). In days past we were slaves, striving for our salvation. Our hire was that we might be commended to God, that we might receive from Him deliverance. But having worked a lifetime, we would still be a servant, a slave, not a son. A slave could work forever, a servant could receive wages forever, and never attain the status of an heir, of a son in the family. But in Christ the gift of sonship is bestowed upon us when we are adopted into the family of God. Not by our poor works do we buy it, gain it, win it, achieve it, but our adoption is something that God does for us. He elevates us out of the status of a slave (a servant striving for freedom) into the glorious inheritance and heritage of a son in the Father's kingdom.

Sometimes truth is stranger than fiction. Years ago there walked down a city street a ragged little newsboy, an orphan urchin, carrying his papers as he walked. In the big city where he lived he passed by a beautiful mansion. The lawn was so neatly kept, the house so impressive, the driveway so inviting. The little lad wandered up the driveway, up to the porch, and before he fully realized what he was doing rang the doorbell. Mr. Lowery, the owner of the spacious home, opened the door and looked down upon the frightened, surprised little fellow. Not knowing what to say, the ragged newsboy blurted out, "Mister, do you have a little boy?" Mr. Lowery, most amused, answered kindly, "No, son, Mrs. Lowery and I do not have any children." The youngster replied in eagerness, "Oh, I'd give everything I own if I could be your little boy and run and play on this beautiful lawn and nobody could drive me away." Then in one of those unusual providences of life, the big man, Mr. Lowery, turned and called upstairs for his wife. The queenly woman walked down the expansive stairway and stood by the side of her husband as he asked, "Dear, would you like to have a little boy?" She quickly replied, "Oh, yes!" The big man turned to the lad and said, "Son, come in, come in." As the little boy walked in that palatial home, the first thing he did was to keep his promise. He reached in his pocket and pulled out thirteen cents and offered the pennies to the big man, saying, "Sir, this is all that I have." We are just like that when we offer to God what little we have and what little we can do to buy our salvation. But the big man took the little boy's hand and closed it around his thirteen pennies and said, "Son, you keep them for I have more than enough for us both." And he took the lad into his house and adopted him, and he became Mr. Lowery's son. That is exactly what God has done for us! We were waifs poor and ragged and outcast, but into the glorious home of our heavenly Father, God has invited us, and bestowed upon us the privilege of sonship. He adopted us into the family of heaven and we are heirs and joint-heirs with Jesus Christ our elder brother. "Wherefore thou art no more a *doulos.*" We are no more slaves, we are no more hirelings, but we are sons, adopted sons, and as sons we are heirs of God through Christ.

The second tremendous privilege that adoption brings to us is that we are no longer under tutors and governors. We are now grown up. We are members of the family. We are accepted in the beloved. We have reached our maturity. Possibly the background of what Paul is saying here is to be found in a custom followed by Roman families. In the days of the Roman empire, when a boy was twenty-five years old, he was given the toga and he became a Roman citizen with all the rights, privileges, and prerogatives pertaining thereto. He was a man, he was a citizen, he had reached his maturity and the young fellow now was a full-fledged Roman citizen, wearing the toga. This is a practice similar to the Jewish Bar Mitzvah. When the lad comes to a certain age, he is accepted then as a man in the family of the Jewish home. So here in Christ we are no longer under types, laws, ordinances, and rituals, but we are now free. We are citizens. We are grown. We are adopted sons. We are co-equals with Christ. We are joint-heirs with Him.

In Galatians 3, the apostle says, "For as many of you as have been baptized into Christ have put on Christ (*enduno,* clothed yourself with Christ)" (v. 27). As the young man in the days of the Roman empire was given a toga to clothe himself as a citizen, so God has given us Christ to clothe ourselves as Christians. We are clothed with the Lord. We have put on Christ. We are fellow-heirs, sons in the household of our Father.

The Christian's Inheritance of the Universe

The third tremendous privilege of adoption is to be seen in the fact that we are heirs of God in Christ. Paul writes in Romans 8 that we are joint-heirs with the Lord. All that God has, all of the riches of His creation are given to us. We are the inheritors of the whole of God's immeasurable kingdom of glory. As sons we join with Christ in the ultimate and final inheritance.

Recently I was riding in a car with a man who had just been converted and baptized as a member of a little Baptist church. In his talking to me he was asking so many questions. His conversion was such a new experience. His new-found faith was so exciting. He had grown up in such a different world. One of the things that he asked me was, "When we die, and when we go to heaven, what are we going to be like in heaven?" I said: "Sometimes I see pictures of a deceased man with wings, with his halo polished, seated on a cloud, doing nothing. Sir, that is a caricature, that is an idiocy. It is an insult to God and the Bible and what God has purposed for us. If there is any one thing which the Scriptures reveal to us it is this, that in heaven we are introduced to an intensive life. All that God in the beginning purposed in the creation, He bestows upon us in the world that is yet to come."

You see, when God made the creation, He gave its administration to Lucifer, the anointed cherub. When Lucifer fell and sin entered the world and creation fell with him, then God recreated a part of that universe and gave its administration, its dominion to Adam. Then God said to Adam, "This is yours, subdue it, dominate it, rule over it." That is why Satan hated him. Outside of Eden's garden gate is that sinister being. He is the envious enemy of man, for God created the man to take over the administration of the whole creation from which Lucifer fell. Adam also fell, but the merciful purpose of God toward the man does not fail, for in Christ all that we lost in Adam we gain in our Saviour. As in Adam we all die, so in Christ are we all made alive. Whatever we were in the beginning, we shall be a thousand times more glorious in the ending, for it is the purpose of God to bestow upon us the administration of the entire universe.

The entire vast, illimitable infinitude of God's creation is ours. There are billions of those Milky Ways, and there are uncounted spheres, suns, stars, and planets. When the ultimate consummation comes, the new Jerusalem will come down from heaven, the golden city of God. But that city is just our home, our address. Our mansion is in the beautiful city, but we shall reign over all of God's universe. We shall go from place to place just as I can do in my mind, from Hong Kong to Alaska to Rio to Afghanistan to India to England. In a moment I can do it. Heaven will be that way. We shall live in that beautiful new Jerusalem home, but we shall administer the whole creation. As God said to one of His servants, "You have been faithful over a little, I am going to make you ruler over five cities." We shall have an intensive life, for we shall inherit with Christ, our joint-heir, the entire universe of God. When people describe heaven as being dull and dreary and lifeless, their description is a thousand miles alien from the purpose and intent and revelation of God. To reign with Christ and to live with Him and with each other is a joy unspeakable. The promise in the Lord is ours forever. We are God's adopted children.

Chapter 15

THE TWO COVENANTS

> Tell me, ye that desire to be under the law, do ye not hear the law?
>
> For it is written, that Abraham had two sons, the one by a bondmaid, the other by a freewoman.
>
> But he who was of the bondwoman was born after the flesh; but he of the freewoman was by promise.
>
> Which things are an allegory: for these are the two covenants; the one from the mount Sinai, which gendereth to bondage, which is Agar.
>
> For this Agar is mount Sinai in Arabia, and answereth to Jerusalem which now is, and is in bondage with her children.
>
> But Jerusalem which is above is free, which is the mother of us all.
>
> For it is written, Rejoice, thou barren that bearest not; break forth and cry, thou that travailest not: for the desolate hath many more children than she which hath an husband.
>
> Now we, brethren, as Isaac was, are the children of promise.
>
> But as then he that was born after the flesh persecuted him that was born after the Spirit, even so it is now.
>
> Nevertheless what saith the scripture? Cast out the bondwoman and her son: for the son of the bondwoman shall not be heir with the son of the freewoman.
>
> So then, brethren, we are not children of the bondwoman, but of the free. (Gal. 4:21-31)

It is God Himself who has made that tremendous distinction and drawn that vast demarcation between grace and law. The two covenants are as different as up and down, as east and west, as light and dark, as fire and water. It is only we who confuse them. God has placed that distinction in the Holy Scriptures clear, lucid, strong. But we are like people who go into a Pantheon and see two gods on opposite sides. In our spiritual illiteracy we seek in confusion to worship them both. But that is not the mind or the revelation or the purpose of God. Law is one thing altogether different, separate and apart from grace. Grace is as fully distinct as God can make it. But there has always been that tendency for those who were saved by grace, by trust, by faith, to go back to seek merit and salvation through the works of the law, through obediences and ordinances, through rituals and ceremonies, through the obeying of commandments. It was so with that Jewish church to whom the Epistle to the Hebrews was addressed. We do not know where it was, but there was a Jewish congregation in the days of the apostles which, having been saved by grace, having found freedom in Christ, sought to return to the yoke and the bondage of the rites, rituals, and ceremonies of the Mosaic legislation. It was confronting the danger of that apostasy that the author wrote the Epistle to the Hebrews. In his appeal the author seeks to bind his readers to the freedom that they have in Christ and not to return to those types, shadows, commandments, and ordinances of the old legislation. Not only was this tendency to return to the law strong among early Jewish Christians, but this letter to the churches of Galatia addressed to Gentiles shows that the same tendency is found among us also. Having found grace in Christ and salvation through trusting in His name, we easily are persuaded to go back under the slavery and the bondage of laws, ordinances, rituals, and ceremonies—observing days and seasons and all the things that pertain to ritualistic, liturgical religion.

Throughout the centuries of days past, we learn that there is nothing that characterizes the human heart and spirit more than this, the longing and affinity for legalistic salvation in religion. However we may be enlightened and illuminated by the Holy Spirit, however we may be regenerated by the presence of God in our hearts, yet there is that human weakness of mind and soul that constantly drags us down and pulls us to the persuasion that we can commend ourselves to God by our good works, that somehow we must merit God's favor, and that somehow in ritual and ceremony and observances we can merit or win our favor with God, that we can be saved by our good works.

The Allegory of Sarah and Hagar, Ishmael and Isaac

In writing to the churches in Galatia, Paul uses an allegory by which he seeks to drive home the truth of the difference between the covenant of the law and the covenant of grace, and to show us that if we are saved by the covenant of the law, we are slaves all the days of our lives. We are never free. But if we are saved by the covenant of grace, we are beyond bondage, we are sons and daughters in the household of the great King, and we are heirs and joint-heirs with Jesus Christ.

In using this story Paul speaks of Abraham, Hagar, Ishmael, Sarah, and Isaac. He says their story is an allegory. He says they represent the two covenants of law and grace. Hagar and her child represent Mount Sinai, which gendereth to bondage, which leads to slavery. "For this Agar is Mount Sinai in Arabia, and answereth to Jerusalem which now is, and is in bondage with her children. But the Jerusalem which is above is free, which is the mother of us all" [and she is Sarah, and her son is Isaac, a child of promise and an heir in the household of those who look in trust and in faith to God] (Gal. 4:25, 26).

Let us recall for a moment the story in Genesis that Paul uses in this allegorical presentation of the difference between the children of the slave woman and the children of the free woman, the difference between our seeking to commend ourselves to God by observing laws, and the way that Christ saves us by trust and by faith. In Genesis 15 Abraham came before the Lord and said, "This Eliezer of Damascus is the heir in my house, and yet you have said to me that one born of my own loins and of the womb of Sarah shall be my heir." God answering took him out under the blue of the skies at night and said to him: "Abraham, can you count those stars? So shall your seed be. He who shall be born out of your loins and the fruit of your wife Sarah shall be your heir." And Abraham believed God and God accounted it to him for righteousness (cf. Gen. 15:2-6).

After that heavenly promise the days passed and multiplied

into years. Abraham is now eighty-six years old and Sarah is seventy-six, and there is no keeping of that promise of God. So according to a depraved custom of that day, Sarah, losing faith and hope, being seventy-six years of age, went to Abraham and said, "I lay in your bosom my slavewoman, Hagar, that you may have a child and an heir by her." Abraham demurred, but Sarah continued to pressure him so Sarah took her slave and laid her in the arms of Abraham and she became his wife. The slave woman conceived and bore a son whom they named Ishmael. That is Genesis 16.

In Genesis 17 God comes to Abraham and tells him that he is to be the father of the promised son and that Sarah will be the mother of the foreordained child. Abraham is ninety-nine years of age. Sarah is eighty-nine years of age. Abraham laughs and says: "Shall he who is a hundred years old be the father of an heir, of a son? And shall Sarah, my wife, who is ninety years of age be the mother of a son?" God replies, "There is nothing too hard for the Lord." And according to the time of life, when Abraham was a hundred years old and Sarah was ninety years old, God gave them the miraculous gift of a son, born of the loins of Abraham, born of the womb of Sarah, and they called his name "Isaac," which means "laughter," "gladness," "rejoicing." God had faithfully kept His promise. That is Genesis 17.

We come now to Genesis 21. When Isaac was weaned, Abraham made a great feast in his household to celebrate the glad occasion. At that feast Ishmael, who was sixteen years of age, mocked and ridiculed and laughed at the little boy Isaac. Sarah, the mother of Isaac, saw it and she said to Abraham: "This slavewoman and her son shall not be heirs with my son. She is to be cast out, she and her son." And though the thing was grievous to Abraham, God said that in the providence and purpose of the Almighty the separation was best. So Hagar, the slavewoman, and Ishmael, the slave son, were sent away and Isaac, the child of faith, became the seed of promise.

Paul uses that story saying that it is an allegory, that it has a powerful and spiritual meaning. The meaning is that Hagar, the slavewoman, and Ishmael, the slaveboy, represent Sinai and the covenant of works, slaves all of their lives. But Sarah, the true wife, and Isaac, the child of promise, represent Calvary and those who find favor and grace in the presence of God through the lovingkindness and forgiveness of Christ our Lord.

The Life and Work of the Slave

We speak first of Hagar. She is a slave and all of her life she remains a slave. She works, and having worked for an entire lifetime, she still works. And her children are slaves. They are in a household paid for what they do. They represent those who seek to be saved by their works, by observing rituals and rites, by being obedient to laws and commandments. They work for a lifetime and still they are slaves. They are still servants. Truly there is no more rigorous taskmaster than the law. It says, "This you ought to do; that is your duty to do; you must do this or else die." And the slaves of the law work, and they work, and they work. They are never done. They are never free. The sinner who seeks to be saved by the law is like a man at a treadmill. Round and round and round he goes. His effort can never cease. The taskmaster cracks the whip, faster and faster and harder and harder he works. But always he is a slave. I think of Samson whose eyes were put out, who was bound, and who at the treadmill went round and round and round until finally he said, "O God, let me die with the Philistines" (cf. Judges 16:21-30). So it is with the man who seeks to keep himself in the favor of God by his own merit. He works and he works and he works. One asks him, "Are you saved?" He says, "I do not know." When he comes to die one asks him, "Are you saved?" He says: 'I do not know. I may not have been good enough. I may not have done it well enough. I just do not know. I cannot know, for I am trying to save myself with works. I am a slave! I never know!" And he dies like that, a slave.

Ishmael represents all legalists, those who seek to commend themselves to God by their good merits. Let us look at him more closely. Ishmael was born first, and that is the way the law is in our lives. When we are children we are like servants. We must be disciplined, we have to be taught, we are under tutors, teachers, and governors. We are no different from a slave.

Again, Ishmael is bigger and rougher and tougher. As it says in the prophecy when he was born: "He shall be a wild man. His hand shall be against every man, and every man's hand shall be against him." So it is with the children of the law. The law is impersonal and inexorable. It knows nothing of faith, of forgiveness, of loving-kindness, of sympathy. The law is tough and rough. When the man in the Book of Numbers was found picking up sticks on the Sabbath Day, the law said stone him, and stone him they did. They took him outside of the camp and buried him under stones until he died. When Achan and his family hid the Babylonish garment and the wedges of silver and gold from the debris and spoils of Jericho, the law said stone them, and stone them they did. That is the law. And when the woman who was taken in sin was brought to the Lord Jesus, the Pharisees said she was to be stoned. The law says so, Moses says so, she is to be stoned—that is the law. The soul that sins shall die! The wages of sin is death! The law is impersonal; it is inexorable. The law condemns, and if one has broken the law, he is under that judgment and under that condemnation.

Another thing about Ishmael: he is a child of the flesh. He is a part of the Jerusalem that now is. He is down here in this earth. He is keeping commandments. He is observing seasons and days. He is following rituals and ceremonies. He is seeking to commend himself to God and to save himself in his own good merit. He is down here in this world; he is a child of flesh. As such, he gets his earthly reward. God does not fail to pay off. He says to the Pharisee that stood where all men could see him pray, "Verily he has his reward." He gets what he wants. The Pharisee who blew the trumpet before Him that the world might see his largess—he got what he wanted, the fame and the notoriety of his liberality. God pays off, but that is all. There is nothing more beyond the wages. The man is still a slave. He is a servant, striving and striving, and at the end of his striving and working, he is paid off. He is a slave, and what shall he do? When he fails, what shall he do? When he sins, what shall he do? When he lacks and falls short, what shall he do? Who can pay that? Who can forgive, who can have mercy? Not the law, for the law to be the law must be impersonal. It is pure justice. Have not you seen that picture of justice with the scales in her hand? Justice is blind. Her eyes are blindfolded. Law is to be impersonal. It cannot take into account any extenuation, mercy, or forgiveness. That is the law. The soul that sins shall die. That is Hagar, the slave mother, and Ishmael, the child of slavery. They represent the covenant of works.

The Life and Work of the Free Born

Sarah and Isaac represent the covenant of grace, the heavenly Jerusalem, the mother of those who are saved by promise, by loving-kindness, by the forgiveness and understanding of the Lord. For you see, it was the purpose of God not through Abarham and Hagar and a slave son to save the world, but it was His purpose through Abraham and Sarah and the child of promise to save the world. Now in our lives the law is first; as children, we are taught, we are trained, we are disciplined. But in God's mind and purpose, grace and mercy were first. Before the foundations of the world were set, Christ, the Lamb of God was crucified. He died, an atonement for our sins in the heart, mind, love, grace, sympathy, mercy, and plan of God before we were born or the world was made. Before God formed you. He saw you; the Lord knew you and loved you in His grace and goodness, and the Lord forgave your sins and adopted you into the family of heaven. Before the law, in fact, four hundred years before the law and before Moses, God said to Abraham, "Your faith is accounted for righteousness." When our first parents fell, God offered atoning blood, and the ground drank it up. There the Lord took the skins of those sacrificed innocent animals and covered the nakedness of our first parents. This is a picture, a harbinger, a type of that ultimate covering (atonement) that can wash our sins away in grace, in love, and in forgiveness.

Sarah is a freewoman. She was always free; she was never a slave. By the side of her husband she lives forever. If one goes to Hebron and to the cave of Machpelah, there after thousands of years one will see the tomb of Abraham and the tomb of Sarah by his side. They are forever one. Sarah is a free woman, and as such she represents the covenant of grace.

She was never a slave, and her child is a free-born child. He is the heir in the family, he is the son of the most high.

Isaac was born miraculously. His birth was a phenomenon of God. His parents were as good as dead. Abraham was a hundred years old; Sarah was ninety years old. That they should have this child of promise is an intervention of God, a miracle of the Lord. God did it. So it is with us. Every man who is adopted into the family of God is a miracle of grace. He is a child of promise. He does not work to attain it. He does not merit it. He is never worthy of it. It is something God does in His grace and mercy. All of the mechanical contrivances of men could not produce that child Isaac. His birth was something God had to do. Culture, ritual, obediences, laws, commandments, education, elevation could not do it. The child of God is born not of blood nor of the will of the flesh nor of the will of man, but of God. He is a child by faith, by grace, and he is received into the family of the Lord as such. He is saved not by himself, not in his worth or merit, but he is saved in the forgiveness, grace, love, and mercy of Jesus.

Isaac was not only miraculously born, gloriously a child of promise, but he was a son, a free-born son. He was never a slave. He was an heir in the family of the great patriarch. We are that kind of an heir. We are joint-heirs with Christ. Jesus and we are the children. He is our elder brother. We are children, sons and daughters of God, with Him. We do not come into the family of God cringing, nor does the Lord God receive us as being convicts and criminals who are pardoned and who are just barely tolerated. We are sons in the family, as loved and as welcomed as God's Son Himself.

When the prodigal son came home, the father did not receive him as "that culprit," "that unworthy scapegoat," "that horrible, incorrigible and obstreperous one," but he was taken back royally. The father said: "Where is the best robe? Clothe him. Where is that marvelous ring? Where is the sign of his sonship? Put it on him. Where are those marvelous shoes, shining with the salvation of the Lord? Put them on him. Let us be happy, let us be glad. Let us sing and rejoice, for this my son was dead and is alive again, he was lost and is found."

And they all began to be merry. That is what it is when we come into the family of God. Not that we are worthy, but *He*, our Lord and Savior is. Not that we do good, but *He* did. Not that we have kept the law, but *He* did. And we are forgiven and loved and welcomed in the mercy, grace, and goodness of God. That is how we are saved. That is how we are welcomed. That is what delivers us beyond any yoke or bondage. Lord, could I ever merit such a blessing, achieve it, be good enough for it? No! I am saved, I am welcomed, I am loved, I am born again, I am adopted, I am an heir, I am a son, by the grace of God and by that grace alone.

The Blessing of Being a Son

Then all of the rest that follows after falls in its order because I am a son. Because I have been saved, I love the Lord. I love to sing about Him, I love to meet with His people, I love to offer Him the dedication and strength and heart and soul of all the issues of life. The born-again life flows Godward and heavenward and Christward.

> Come, ye sinners, poor and needy,
> Weak and wounded, sick and sore;
> Jesus ready stands to save you,
> Full of pity, love, and pow'r.
>
> Come, ye weary, heavy-laden,
> Lost and ruined by the fall;
> If you tarry till you're better,
> You will never come at all.
>
> I will arise and go to Jesus,
> He will embrace me in His arms;
> In the arms of my dear Saviour,
> Oh, there are ten thousand charms.

Not by works of righteousness which we have done, but according to His mercy, His grace, His loving-kindness, His forgiveness does He save us. How do I know that I am saved? Because I have kept the law? No. Because I have done good deeds? No. Because I have observed the rituals? No. How do I know that I am saved? Because the Lord promised that if I would trust Him, he would see me through. If I believe on Him, I will have everlasting life, and I am believing God who could not lie to keep His promise. That is the way I am saved. That is the way all of us are saved. It is in the grace and goodness of God that we become children of the covenant, of Calvary. Will you accept that grace, love, mercy, pardon, and forgiveness? Come with us and walk with us as the free-born children of God.

Chapter 16

FAITH AND FREEDOM

> Stand fast therefore in the liberty wherewith Christ hath made us free, and be not entangled again with the yoke of bondage.
> Behold, I Paul say unto you, that if ye be circumcised, Christ shall profit you nothing.
> For I testify again to every man that is circumcised, that he is a debtor to do the whole law.
> Christ is become of no effect unto you, whosoever of you are justified by the law; ye are fallen from grace.
> For we through the Spirit wait for the hope of righteousness by faith.
> For in Jesus Christ neither circumcision availeth any thing, nor uncircumcision; but faith which worketh by love.
> Ye did run well; who did hinder you that ye should not obey the truth?
> This persuasion cometh not of him that calleth you.
> I have confidence in you through the Lord, that ye will be none otherwise minded: but he that troubleth you shall bear his judgment, whosoever he be.
> And I, brethren, if I yet preach circumcision, why do I yet suffer persecution? then is the offence of the cross ceased.
> For, brethren, ye have been called unto liberty; only use not liberty for an occasion to the flesh, but by love serve one another.
> For all the law is fulfilled in one word, even in this; Thou shalt love thy neighbour as thyself.
> (Gal. 5:1-8, 10, 11, 13, 14)

For just a moment of review, let us recall the circumstances that surounded the establishment of the churches in Galatia. When the Apostle Paul on his first missionary journey preached the Gospel to the inhabitants of the Roman province of Galatia in the center of Asia Minor, his message was wondrously received. Out of heathenism, paganism, and idolatry these people turned to Christ and were gloriously saved. They received the gift of the Spirit by faith. While they were rejoicing in the Lord and the presence of the moving spirit of Jesus among them and in them, there came Judaizers who said to them that to believe in Christ is well and good but such a faith alone cannot save you. One must add to faith all the works of the law. The response of the apostle was vehement. It was immediate. It was thunderous. For example, in the passage that I just read he says in 5:1, "You who would go back under the law are becoming entangled again with the yoke of bondage." In verse 2, "You who would keep the law in order to be saved, verily Christ shall profit you nothing." Verse 3: "You who would be justified by the law, truly you are a debtor to it, a slave to it, all the days of your life. And after you have slaved under it you still do not know whether you are saved or not." Verse 4, "You who would be saved by personal merit and obedience to the law, Christ is become of no effect unto you. There is no need for Him. He is extraneous and peripheral." Verse 5, "You who would be saved by ceremonies and rituals and man's devices and obediences to commandments, verily the hope of righteousness by faith is lost. It has atrophied; it ceases to exist." In verse 6 he sums up the whole meaning of the Christian faith: "it is "the faith which worketh by love." This is the definition of the whole message of Christianity.

With one sweep of his hand Paul would brush aside the whole man-made device of man's attempt to save himself. Whether it is keeping rituals and ceremonies, or whether it is obediences to laws or commandments, all of it does the apostle sweep away and he thus brings us to the one revelation of salvation we find in the Word of God, which is through faith in Jesus Christ.

The Kind of Faith That Saves the Soul

What kind of faith is it that saves our souls from sin and delivers us to God and salvation? First, it is not mere intellectual assent to the reality of God and the Holy Scriptures. It is something different from intellectual perception and acknowledgment. James, the pastor of the church in Jerusalem, in the second chapter of his letter says, "You believe in God? well, good, the devils also believe, and they tremble" (see v. 19). The demons know all about the faith. They know it more intimately and powerfully than we do. But we are not saved by knowledge, by intellectual assent. Saving faith is not mere perception and understanding. I can talk about the Lord, write books about the Lord, sing about the Lord, preach about the Lord, discuss the Lord, be knowledgeable in the things of the Lord, and still be lost.

Second, this saving faith is not the recitation of creeds. "I believe in God the Father Almighty, Maker of heaven and earth . . ." etc. It is not a truth that we can take out, put back, and shuffle around like a piece of paper.

Third, this saving faith is not joining an organization, a church, a philanthropic group, a fraternity. The faith that saves is something in an altogether different world. One time I bowed my head in the presence of the Lord, and asked of God: "Lord, when You say in the Book, 'Whosoever believeth in him should not perish, but have everlasting life,' what is it thus to believe? What is saving faith? The devils believe and tremble. The acknowledgment of the facts and truth of Christ on the part of many has been known and published through the centuries, but that does not save. What is this saving faith?" And as I asked of the Lord, there came to my heart that passage that Paul wrote in 2 Timothy 1:12, "For I know whom I have believed, and am persuaded that he is able to keep that which I have committed unto him against that day." Saving faith is a commitment of your life to Christ. It is the handing over, the turning over, of your soul to Him. Faith that saves is a trusting in Christ. What must I do to be saved? Believe *in* the Lord Jesus, *on* the Lord Jesus, *upon* the Lord Jesus, and you will be saved (see Acts 16:31).

Did you ever get into a plane and notice that the door to the cockpit was open? Did you ever look through that door at those hundreds of instruments on the panel? Sometimes I am in one of those powerful planes 39,000 feet in the air. What would I do if the landing of the plane were dependent upon me? I know not a single instrument on the panel. I know not a single knob to move, button to punch, or lever to turn. If the safety of the plane depended upon me, I would surely die. I am forced to trust that pilot completely, implicitly. Because I trust him, I sit there in the plane in perfect confidence that he will bring it to land. Saving faith is a like trust in Christ and commitment to Him.

Did you ever have an operation? How completely do you lay your life into the hands of the physician! While you are under an anesthetic and thus unconscious, you must trust the doctor completely. You must commit your life into his hands. That is saving faith when we place our lives into the hands of Christ.

Fourth, this saving faith is not only the committal of our lives to the Lord Jesus, it is not only full trust in Christ, but it is also the abandonment of any hope of any kind in anyone else or in any other way. It is renouncing all other hope save in Him. It is a resignation of ourselves to Christ. There is nothing else to save us, there is no one else to turn to. Remember what the Lord said to His apostles, "Will ye also go away?" and Simon Peter answered for the Twelve: "Lord, to whom shall we go? Thou hast the words of eternal life and we believe and are sure that Thou art the Christ, the Son of God that should come into the world." Saving faith is the abandonment of any other hope save in Christ.

> On Christ, the solid Rock, I stand;
> All other ground is sinking sand.
>
> My hope is built on nothing less
> Than Jesus' blood and righteousness;
> I dare not trust the sweetest frame,
> But wholly lean on Jesus' name.
>
> When He shall come with trumpet sound,
> Oh, may I then in Him be found;
> Dressed in His righteousness alone,
> Faultless to stand before the throne.
>
> On Christ, the solid Rock, I stand;
> All other ground is sinking sand.

That is the faith that saves.

Why God Chose Faith as the Way of Salvation

Why did God choose that way for us to be saved? Answer one, because there is no other way possible. There is no alternative. It is that or nothing beside. Look, if I seek to save myself by merit, by self-righteousness, what shall I do with my sins in the past? If I seek to save myself by my merit and self-righteousness, what shall I do with my sins in the future? If I stand here and avow before God, "From this moment on I shall live perfectly, sinlessly, virtuously; there shall be no error or mistake in my life . . . ," if I swear before God that from this moment on I shall live in His presence perfectly, I know I cannot keep that oath. Error will attend my way and mistake and sin dog my path as long as I live in this carnal body. What shall I do about my sins of the future? And what can I do with my sins of the past? Somewhere, some day, somehow, if I am ever to be saved, I must cast myself upon the mercies, goodnesses, and forgiveness of God. There is no other way. Job cried in the seventh chapter of his book, "I have sinned, what shall I do?" And the Apostle Paul admitted in Romans 7: "O wretched man that I am! What I would do I don't do. What I don't do I would do. Wretched man that I am, who shall deliver me from the body of this death?" Somewhere, sometimes, somehow, some day, if I am ever saved, it must be in the mercy and forgiveness and goodness of God. There is no other way.

Answer two, why does God choose this way of faith in order that we might be saved? Because herein God shows Himself and reveals Himself as being merciful, redemptive, gracious, and full of loving-kindness and tender mercy. In Genesis 1 and 2 we have the creative work of God revealed. No man was there to see the creation in the beginning. The story had to come by revelation. God thus reveals Himself in Genesis 1 and 2 as being the great, mighty Creator. Think of someone who could just speak worlds into existence, produce the whole creation by fiat! "Let it be," and there it is. Light shines, the stars are placed into their orbits, the earth is formed, and God glorifies the whole creation with beauty, wonder, and amazement. Oh, the revelation of God in Genesis 1 and 2! But there is more to God than just the *pantokrator*, the mighty Creator. Beginning in chapter 3, and for the rest of the Bible, God reveals Himself as being redemptive, merciful, full of loving-kindness, tenderness, and graciousness. That is why our salvation is not by our works but is received as a gift from His kind and gracious hands. "For by grace are ye saved through faith; and that not of yourselves: it is the gift of God: not of works, lest any man should boast" (Eph. 2:8, 9), lest he should say: "I did it. I bought it. I won it." Our salvation is a gift of God. It reveals the gracious, merciful, redemptive heart of the Almighty.

Answer three, why does God choose to save us by faith, by trust? Not only because there is no other way (if we are ever saved it is because He is merciful to us), not only is it because God chose to bestow it upon us as a gift that we might know Him as a gracious and merciful God, but also our salvation through faith is suitable and is suited for all of us poor, dying sinners. Would you say to a dying man, "Do this, do these works, and thou shalt live"? He is a dying man; he cannot do them. How could he, then, be saved? That is why the Lord said in John 3:14, 15 that the Gospel of salvation is like a dying man looking at the raised, brazen serpent in the wilderness. "And as Moses lifted up the serpent in the wilderness, even so must the Son of man be lifted up: That whosoever believeth in him should not perish, but have eternal life." Less could not be asked. More by some could not have been offered. The man is dying. He has been struck by a venomous, poisonous snake and he is dying. What would you say to a dying man that he do and be saved? That man in the wilderness who was struck by a venomous snake and is dying is a type and a picture of all of us. We are a dying people. What do you say to a dying man that he be saved? In the wilderness the Gospel was, "Look and live, look to Jesus Christ and live!" It is suited for us dying sinners that we be saved by trust and by faith.

Answer four, why does God choose to save us by faith? Not only because it is suitable, but also because it provides an open door to all mankind—to the helpless, to the hopeless, to the unknowing, to the untaught, to be untrained, to the old, to the young. There is no group, there is no one but to whom God opens the door of salvation through faith. If He said, "Buy it," there are some of us so poor we could never pay for it. If He said, "Keep these laws, be perfect, and be saved," there is none of us that knows how to be perfect. Whatever requirement God would make there would be some of us who could not equal it. But when God says, "Trust, look, believe, accept, take, receive," then any of us can respond.

I have preached the Gospel in the heart of darkest Africa, in the Indian subcontinent, in Indonesia, on the borders of China, in the isles of the sea, and around the earth. I have seen people untrained, untaught (having lived their lives in the darkness of ignorance and superstition), come out of the depths of hopelessness into the light of the glory of the Gospel of the Son of God just by looking to Jesus. The Gospel message of trust is an open door to all of us. To the man who can do nothing but just look, just receive, to him God mediates the marvelous gift of eternal life. What could the thief, the malefactor who was nailed to the cross by the side of Jesus, what could he do? He turned his face toward the central cross, to the dying Savior, and said, "Lord, when thou comest into thy kingdom, remember me." His word of trust and his word of faith were enough. He was saved, for the Lord Himself said, "This day shalt thou be with me in paradise." God chose that way of salvation by faith because it is open to any one of us. It is suited for us dying sinners. It reveals the goodness and graciousness of God. It is a gift from His hand. And there is no other alternative. If we are ever saved it is because of the goodness, mercy, and the forgiveness of God.

Faith as a Motive for True Righteousness

Let us now consider how that saving faith operates, the method of its working. For one thing, when we are saved, we become a someone else. We become a new creation. We are in the Lord someone different. We are not the same anymore. It is a new life. It is a new love. It is a new heart. It is a new day. It is a new vision. It is a new hope. Second Corinthians 5:17 says "Therefore if any man be in Christ, he is a new creature: old things are passed away, behold, all things are become new." When a man is saved, when he gives his heart to Christ, he is someone else. He is a different someone. You do not change a man by law and by regulation. An illustration of the inability of the legislature to change the heart can be seen in attempted liquor legislation. If we passed a law to close down all bars, saloons, and liquor establishments (and that would be good because it would eliminate the advertising of liquor and put it out of the sight of those who walk up and down the street), when that is done and the hearts of the people are not changed, do you know where you will find the saloon? Do you know where you will find the bar and the brewery? You will find it in the home. You will find the bar inside the house. When a man is in Christ he is a new creation. He is someone else. He is a different kind of individual. He has a different interest. He has a different love. He has a different heart. He has a different soul. He has a different outlook. He is someone else.

Second, the saved man has a new and a different motive. When a man seeks to save himself by the keeping of commandments, he lives under the fear all of his life that if he does not keep the law just right he will be damned. What he does, therefore, he does out of the motive of fear, of damnation, hell, and judgment. He lives like a slave all the days of his life. There is, however, a greater motive for righteousness and a more powerful one. Look at this passage in Romans 13: "For this, Thou shalt not commit adultery (that is a commandment), Thou shalt not kill (that is a commandment), Thou shalt not steal (that is a commandment), Thou shalt not bear false witness (that is a commandment), Thou shalt not covet (that is a commandment); and if there be any other commandment, it is briefly comprehended in this saying, namely, Thou shalt love thy neighbour as thyself (vv. 9, 10). Here the apostle is speaking to all mankind and for all that it means in the admonition, "Love thy neighbour as thyself." Let us examine that motive for just a moment.

While preaching these messages I had been bombarded by someone who listened to me preach (and I am grateful that he listened), I'd been bombarded by letters from somebody who had been listening to me as I preached through the Book of Galatians and sarcastically, sardonically, and contemptuously he wrote to me and said: "So we are saved and therefore we are free, free, (he underscored 'free'). We are not under the law. According to what you have been preaching we are free." Whoever the critic was, he was a crude, rude, carnal, lustful sort of fellow, so he further wrote: "So I'm free! Wonderful, wonderful. I will sleep with a different woman every night." That was one of his illustrations in a letter to me. I apologize to you for quoting from it, but I need to drive home the point that Paul is making here. Paul makes no apologies about what he says; neither do I. "Fine," says this man, "I am free. I will sleep with a different woman every night. I'm not under commandments. I am free. I'll do that every night." All right, let us look at the motive that lies back of a righteousness by faith through love. Suppose that carnal fellow fell in love with a wonderful girl. Suppose he asked her to be his wife and suppose she gave her life to him. If he really loved her, would he like to sleep with a different woman every night? Would he? If he really loved her, would he like to break her heart and destroy her faith and her love and her life? What about that motive of love? It is stronger than death. Many waters cannot quench it.

Now, let us take the next commandment, "Thou shalt not kill." Here is a man who has befriended you. He has been kind to you. What do you do in love to repay him? You stab him in the back or you shoot him through the heart! Could you? Or, take the next commandment, "Thou shalt not steal." You have a boy that you love and the boy wants to go to college but you do not have any money for the lad to go to school. The boy, therefore, works hard to save money to go to school (I know all about that—wanting an education, wanting to go to school—and too poor to go). The boy works hard. He is your boy. You love the boy. But you steal the money that he makes! Could you? You tell me that love is not a more dynamic motive for righteousness than judgmental law? If the man loved the boy he could not do it. And if there be any other commandment there is no motive so central, so dynamic in this earth as the motive of a devoted love, a commitment of life. The Lord knows, the Lord sees, and when you give your life to Him, oh, what a change in wanting, in desiring, in values! The whole earth is different for you are different. This is the dynamic of love that Paul speaks of here. A moment ago we quoted from Romans. The apostle writes the same thing again here in Galatians 5:14, "For all the law is fulfilled in one word, even in this; Thou shalt love thy neighbor as thyself." Love does no ill to anyone. If I love you truly, I will want to help you and encourage you and be a blessing to you. I do not want to hurt you. I do not want to hinder you. I do not want to break your heart or your life if I love you.

The Creation of a New Relationship to God

The method of faith—not only is it the gift of a new heart and a new life, and not only is it the portraying of a new motive, but also it creates a new relationship. I am no longer in the father's house as a slave, trying to win a reward, a stipend, earn a salary, and when I have slaved and worked all my life I am still at the end of the day a slave, a servant, still working for money. But by faith in Christ I am adopted into the family of God. I am a son. I am a fellow-heir with the Lord and what I do, I do not do for pay, for reward, or for money like a slave, but what I do now, I do because I am a child of the King, I am a son of heaven. I am a joint-heir with Jesus Christ. I belong to the family of God, and as such I am free. In John 8 the Lord said, "Verily, verily, I say unto you Whosoever committeth sin is the servant of sin. . . . If the Son therefore shall make you free, ye shall be free indeed" (vv. 8:34, 36). We are not slaving to be accepted of God; we are not living in fear lest we have not merited the favor of the Lord. We are free! We are sons and daughters of the great King and what we do now we do to bless and honor the name of our heavenly Father. This is what we want to do. We are joint-heirs with Christ and as such the adoration and the praise of our lives flow fully and heavenward toward Him. We do not go to church by commandment. All my life I have loved to go to church. I do not sing these songs by commandment. All of my life I have loved to sing these praises. I do not associate with Christian people out of commandment, by law; rather, I love to be with Christian people. This is the blessing and the favor and the glory of God upon those who come to Christ by faith. We are not under a whip, we are not under coercion, we are not under commandment. Rather out of a free spirit we come before the Lord.

O God, in the fullness of my soul I bow in Thy presence, I praise Thy blessed name; and if God were to give me a thousand lives, all thousand of them, Lord, would I use to glorify and to worship and to adore and to praise Thee. I would rather be a Christian than anything else in the earth. I have it in my heart to love God because I am saved. He has spoken to me and I have heard His voice and answered with my life. Will you do that?

Chapter 17

THE OFFENSE OF THE CROSS

> And I, brethren, if I yet preach circumcision, why do I yet suffer persecution? then is the offence of the cross ceased.
> (Gal. 5:11)

In Galatians 5:11 we find these words, "...then is the offence of the cross ceased." The Greek word in the text for "offence" is *scandalon*. "Then is the *scandalon* (and the English word 'scandal' comes from it) of the cross ceased." We have met that word before in 1 Corinthians 1:22 ff., where Paul wrote: "For the Jews require a sign, and the Greeks seek after wisdom: But we preach Christ crucified, unto the Jews a stumblingblock, and unto the Greeks foolishness; But unto them which are called, both Jews and Greeks, Christ the power of God, and the wisdom of God." In that text is the word, "offence." "The Jews require a sign, and the Greeks seek after wisdom: But we preach Christ crucified, unto the Jews a *scandalon*, 'offence,' here translated 'stumblingblock.'" The Gospel message to the Jews was a *scandalon*. To the Greeks it was *morion*, "idiocy," "foolishness," "moronic." But unto us who are saved it is Christ the "dunamis," the "power" of God.

That word, the *scandalon* of the cross, the offense of the cross, aptly described the attitude of the enemies of the Christian faith toward the cross of Christ. The Judaizers against whom Paul is addressing this letter to the churches in Galatia were most content to name and to accept Jesus as a great man, a good man. His words of mercy, His deeds of forgiveness, His kindness, His compassion, all were beautifully acceptable, but as a way of salvation His cross was a *scandalon*. It was an offense, it violated the properties of life. For a man to be saved by rituals, ceremonies, obediences to commandments and the keeping of laws was perfectly reasonable and natural and one that they promulgated, but that a man could be saved by trusting the Christ of the cross was a *scandalon.* The offensiveness of the execution of Christ!

The Cross as It Is Accepted Today

This letter to Galatia represents a day of nineteen hundred years ago. Is the cross a *scandalon,* an offense today? How things have changed! The cross today is looked upon as a part of the culture of western civilization. In many instances men build churches on the plan of the cross: there is the nave, the trancepts, and the central altar in the apse. The cross is placed high on the top of our tallest steeples as the sign and the aegis under which we are proud to march. The cross is embossed on our Bibles. It is a piece of jewelry, worn as an ornament around our necks. It is used in the ecclesiastical decoration of all the churches of Christendom. It is an object of art. Even the poet who may not at all have any conversance with the faith will use the cross as an acceptable image in his poetic lines. The whole world has come to accept the cross as a sentimental sign of dedication and self-sacrifice.

Is the cross offensive today? Actually, this day is no different than the day of the Apostle Paul. The same offensiveness, the same *scandalon,* that was found in the cross in the day of the apostles is no less true in our day and in our generation. It was with keen insight that Isaiah said "He hath no form nor comeliness, and when we shall see him, there is no beauty that we should desire him" (Isa. 53:2b). In that same vein Paul wrote these words, "For the preaching of Christ crucified is to the Jew an offence and to the Greek it is moronic idiocy" (cf. 1 Cor. 1:23). Today, as in that day, the beautiful life of Jesus is as perfume. To follow the Lord around the shores of Galilee, to look upon the Christ of the Sermon of the Mount or the Christ of the golden rule or the Christ of the compassionate, forgiving Savior, or the Christ of superlative pedagogical wisdom is acceptable. But actually the Christ of the cross is as scandalous, as offensive, today as it was then.

Interesting to me was a story that happened in the days

of Thomas Carlyle. He was in London and the guest of a glittering socialite. She was light of mind, one of those butterflies that lives on the surface, sipping here, sipping there. In the course of the conversation she began to speak of the guilt of the Jewish people in slaying the Son of God, the Savior of the world. She said that if Christ were to come today we would open our homes to Him and welcome Him. Then she said to Mr. Carlyle, "Do you not agree?" The great Scot essayist replied (and I copied down his answer): "No, I do not agree, madame. I think that had He come very fashionably dressed with plenty of money and preaching doctrines most palatable to the higher orders, I might have had the honor of receiving a card from you on the back of which would be written 'to meet our Saviour.' But if He came uttering His sublime precepts and denouncing the Pharisees and associating with publicans as He did, you would have treated Him much as the Jews did and cried out, 'Take Him to Newgate and hang Him!" It is quite problematical whether if the Lord came today that He would be any more generously received or more devoutly believed in, accepted, than He was in the days of the Apostle Paul, for the offense of the cross, the *scandalon* of the cross, is not ceased.

How can such a thing be said in the cultured society in which we live and in the manifest degree of civilization into which we have advanced? There are three answers that explain why the cross is a *scandalon*, an offence, today, yesterday, in the generation that is yet to come, and throughout the centuries of human story.

The Cross as an Exposition of the True Nature and Character of the World

Reason number one, the cross is an offense because it exposes the real nature and heart of the world. Cheap sentimentality deifies humanity and glosses over the iniquity and the wickedness in the human heart. The cross opens our real nature to public view.

It was interesting to me to read about a famous church in Edinburgh in which one minister preached at the morning hour and another minister preached at the evening hour, both of them fellow pastors of the church. The man who stood up at the morning hour said that there is an inherent veneration for goodness in the heart of man. If virtue and goodness were to appear it would immediately be enthroned and received in adoration on the part of all mankind. At the evening hour his fellow minister, apparently unaware of what the other one had said in the morning hour, said, "Moral goodness and beauty of life and character came incarnate into this world and instead of being enthroned, humanity took Him, mocked Him, ridiculed Him, finally nailed Him to a cross, and He died in shame on a tree." Which one of those two ministers was correct? History says it was the second minister who really portrayed the depth of the depravity of the human heart. All we need to do is to read the pages of history and especially the pages of the Bible to confirm that judgment upon the human race.

In Genesis 6 it says, "And God saw that the wickedness of man was great in the earth, and that every imagination of the thoughts of his heart was only evil continually" (v. 5). And the rest of the story verifies that judgment from heaven. The story of Israel and the story of Judah is one of constant relapse into sin. The story of Nineveh and the story of Babylon is one of ruthless, merciless cruelty. The story of the whole human race is summariezd in the first chapter of the Book of Romans. I do not read it in public; I never heard of anyone reading it in public. Yet it is a characterization of the Roman Empire and Roman civilization. It sounds like a description of the morality in America today. But as terrific an indictment of the human race as we find in the pages of secular history, there is no exposing such as we find in the crucifixion and the cross of the Son of God. John 20 says that He was hanged, He was nailed to the tree outside the city wall, outside the city gate on the main highway that leads into Jerusalem. The multitudes passed by. They saw the pain and they heard the crying and the sobs of the Son of God. Yet they looked upon His tears in silent indifference.

That cross is a rebuke to the entire human race. It is a rebuke to Herod Antipas with his coarse vices and his cheap revelry; to Caiphas, the scheming high priest; to Pontius Pilate, the Roman governor with his eye on his career and his place; to Judas Iscariot with his covetous, traitorous deeds; to the Roman soldiers, gambling at the foot of the cross for His fifth garment; to the Pharisees, the Scribes, the leaders of the religion of the nation as they mocked Him; to the throngs as they sat down in indifference or passed by in silent unconcern; even to the disciples themselves as they forsook Him and fled; and to Simon Peter as he denied three times that he ever knew Him. Like the shadow of the wings of the death angel that passed over Egypt in the night of the Passover, the shadow of depravity covers the whole human race. The crucifixion of Christ was a judgment upon the city, upon the state, upon the empire, and upon all humanity. And we are no different! The sin and the violence of which mankind is capable is without measure.

The Cross as a Call to Self-denial and Repudiation of the Rewards of the World

Reason number two, the offense of the cross, the *scandalon* of the cross is no less so today because it is a call to self-denial and a repudiation of the rewards of the world. One can see that pointedly in the life of the rich young ruler. He was noble in every respect. He had kept the commandments, he told the Lord, from the days of his youth, from his youth up. And the Lord looking upon him loved him. He was the epitome of worldly success. The rewards and the emoluments of the social order had been heaped upon him. He was rich, he was young, and he was a ruler. When he asked the Lord concerning the eternal life preached by the prophet of Galilee, the Lord said to him: "There is not room enough, the way is not wide enough, for a man to go into heaven with his heart bound up in what he possesses. Get rid of the excess baggage. Give it away. It is trash. It is nothing. Get rid of it." And the next sentence says, "Come, take up your cross and follow Me." The Scriptures say that the lad was sad at that saying and went away grieved, for he had great possessions. Ah, how different does Christ look at things and does Christ look at the world in contrast to how the world looks at itself. In the last chapter of Paul's last letter he said, "Demas hath forsaken me, having loved this present world" (2 Tim. 4:10).

Oh, I grant you it is romantically interesting to follow in the steps of the Teacher along the blue shores of the Galilee.

It would be most interesting to join the parade of Palm Sunday and enter into the City of Peace, into Jerusalem, in the day of the triumph of our Lord. But to take His cross and to go outside of the city bearing His reproach is a *scandalon* and an offense. It is something different.

For example, who wants to be a prude? And who wants to be a square? Who wants to be looked upon as Puritanical and Victorian? We have the desire to be set forth and to be accepted, and, if one is young enough, to be popular. I sat at a civic meeting here in Dallas. Strange thing to me, it was supposed to be a religious meeting, one of these affairs that Dallas presents as pulling all of the community together back of a common philanthrophy. Well, I was seated in a big ballroom between two laymen. I was the pivot man in between. On one side and on the other side they talked about their drinking, their gambling, their promiscuous whoremongering, back and forth. And I, a minister, was expected to be a good sport. Why should I think anything of their gambling? Why should I say anything about their drinking? Why should I think anything of their whoremongering? After all, we all are to be good sports. Who wants to be prudish or square or Puritanical or Victorian? At the end of the meal I said to the men, "Before I leave I would just like for you to know that my heart is not in sympathy with anything that you men have discussed and joked about at this dinner meeting today."

The politician wants to be known as a good sport. He does not want to be a square, Puritanical, or prudish. What would the brewery, the distillery, the pimp, the gambler, and the bookie say about a puritanical politician? The liquid pot industry is infiltrating into every legislative hall in the land. The politician in order to be a good sport says "damn" and "hell" and he drinks and he gambles a little. That is what it is to be accepted by the world. The *scandalon,* the offense of the cross is overwhelming!

Take anything that the world prizes. Name it. Look upon the man who is acceptable in our culture and in our society. What kind of a man is he? He is a man of success. He is affluent. He has all of the accouterments of wealth. As such he is to be respected and admired. Those are the standards of the world. The Lord is so different! What the world had to offer was nothing to Him. And the followers of Jesus who most sincerely live in the Spirit of our Lord are those who have that same persuasion in their hearts concerning the blandishments, the rewards, the stipends, the accumulations, and the embellishments of the world. In themselves accumulations are nothing, nothing at all. They do not even weigh in the balance.

There was a shabbily dressed man who lived on his small salary in a little house. He was known as being stingy, penurious, and frugal. The pastor ate dinner, a sparse meal, with that shabbily dressed man in his humble little cottage. The pastor was astonished to learn that that humble man had taken his little salary and had tried to live on as small a part of it as he could, and with the rest of his salary he had supported a misisonary on the foreign field. Was this man a worldly success? Who would want to emulate his poverty? Look at his dress! Look at his success! Look at the house that he lives in! Look at him! Who would follow that? Truly, there is such a difference between how God sees a thing and how the world regards it. Why, I can remember a deacon of many years ago who had served in my church for a generation. He came to church on a bicycle. In his old age a car struck and killed him while he was riding his bicycle. I buried him. He gave every penny he possessed to the church. I am not saying that one ought to do that nor am I implying that to be a true follower of Christ we must give all our living to the work of our Lord. The Lord never told Zacchaeus to sell everything he had. The Lord did not say that to Nicodemus or to Joseph of Arimathaea, both of whom were wealthy men. I am merely pointing out that in our sight, in our judgment, sometimes what we think is tremendous success in God's sight is a peccadillo. It is inconsequential or insignificant. Some things that we regard as so despised and rejected may be in God's sight prized beyond measure. The *scandalon* of the cross is a call to self-denial and a repudiation of the cheap rewards of the world.

The Cross as the Only Way of Salvation

Third, why the offense of the cross, the *scandalon* of the cross? Because it is presented in the Bible, in the Word of God, in the preaching of the Gospel of Christ as the *only* way of salvation. It is presented thus openly, pointedly, vehemently, vigorously. There is no doubt of the clarity of the message of the Word of God regarding the way to be saved. It is *the* truth, it is *the* way, it is *the* life, and there is none other. It is as Simon Peter stood up and proclaimed, "Neither is there salvation in any other: for there is none other name under heaven given among men, whereby we must be saved" (Acts 4:12). Oh, when the Gospel message is presented as the Bible and the Holy Scriptures present it, it is always that. It is not Christ possibly. It is not Christ alternatively. It is not Christ among many others. It is the Lord Christ alone and that is an offense, and a *scandalon* to most of the world.

Why is the world offended at the way of salvation? There is only a small minority in the world that does not believe that there are many ways to heaven. They say we are all striving to get to the same place. The Buddhist goes his way, the Mohammedan goes his way, the Shintoist goes his way, the Confucianist goes his way, the Taoist goes his way, and all of the other faiths go their way, and among them the Christian goes his way. We are all striving for the same thing and going to the same place. They say that if a man is sincere in his Judaism, or sincere in his Islamic faith, or in the veneration of his ancestors, as is a good Confucianist, or whatever he is, he is just as certain of heaven and as certain to be saved as the Christian who looks in faith to the blood of Christ. This attitude is almost universally accepted. When the Christian, therefore, stands up and says there is no other way to heaven and there is no other message by which we can be saved than the cross of Jesus Christ, his faith becomes a *scandalon* and an offense.

Even the liberal ministers deny the effect, the cleansing, the atoning power of the blood of Christ. Such a bloody way of salvation is unthinkable to their sensitive souls. They refer to it as a "butcher's block" religion and a "religion of the shambles." I have been in churches where all of the hymn books were purged of songs on the blood. To the liberal minister Christ is a good man. He is a heroic man. He is an ideal man. But He is not in any wise looked upon in this liberal world as being the Savior who cleanses up through His blood. That is an offense to modern culture and society.

It has always been interesting to me how the Christian faith is uncompromising in its proclamation that the way of salvation is *Christ* and nothing else! There is no alternative. It is Christ or it is nothing. Believing in Him we are saved. Refusing Him we are lost.

The Roman Empire was the most tolerant, the most liberal, the most wise, and the most accurate in its handling of the many provinces and religions of its empire of any kingdom that ever existed. Men could worship, have temples, and do as they pleased. And yet the Roman Empire and the Caesars persecuted the Christians. Why? For one simple reason: the Christian refused to compromise his faith with any other religion whatsoever. When the Romans invited them to place Jesus in their Pantheon beside Jupiter, by the side of Juno, by the side of Neptune, by the side of Isis, by the side of Osiris, the Christian flatly refused. It is Christ alone. When the Christians were invited just to bow down before the Roman image, their lives could be spared if they would merely take a pinch of incense and put it on the fire that burned in the presence of the image of the Roman Caesar. The Christian died rather than compromise with a pinch of incense. I am telling you what is the faith of the New Testament, the faith of the martyrs, and the faith of the true men of God through the centuries. That kind of a faith is uncompromising. There is no salvation in any other.

The depraved heart of humanity does not change. We may have learned in some intsances to be a little astute in how we address our violence. Years ago it may have been with an ax, a stone, or a club. It may have been with an arrow and a spear or with a musket and a rifle. Men are more sophisticated today. We do the same violence with a jet bomber or with dynamite or with hell-bombs. But the depravity of the human heart is just the same. The offense of the cross and the *scandalon* of the message of Christ ultimately is no more acceptable today than it was in the generations that have passed. Nor will it be more accetpable in the generations that are yet to come, until the Lord returns from heaven and brings righteousness to the war-weary, sin-cursed earth.

Dear God, help us through these unfolding years. Master, let there be less and less of us and more and more of Thee until there be none of us and all of Thee. Lord, help us in our judgment to see things as they really are. Help us not to be blinded by the tinsel, tinfoil, and the cheap glitter of the world, but to see things as those who endure, looking upon the invisible. Grant it, God, please.

Chapter 18

THE RESPONSIVE HEART

> But the fruit of the Spirit is love, joy, peace, longsuffering, gentleness, goodness, faith,
> Meekness, temperance: against such there is no law.
> And they that are Christ's have crucified the flesh with the affections and lusts.
> If we live in the Spirit, let us also walk in the Spirit.
> Let us not be desirous of vain glory, provoking one another, envying one another. (Gal. 5:22-26)

The message of these verses speaks of the motivation of the life of liberty apart from the coercive, oppressive demands of the law. We see this motivation plainly in the text: "But the fruit of the Spirit is love, joy, peace, longsuffering, gentleness, goodness, faith, meekness, temperance: against such there is no law." Law has no part or place in it. "If we live in the Spirit," and we do under God, "let us also walk in the Spirit," and we shall with His help and grace.

The life of obedience unto the law is always one accompanied by defeat and frustration. The man who seeks to commend himself to God by doing good, the man who seeks to save his soul by observing rituals and commandments, is a man who continually lives in the abysmal depths of fear, dread, and insecuirty. "Do this and thou shalt live, do not do this and thou shalt be damned," is the simple precept of the law, but the man never knows whether he is doing it well enough to be saved and he is constantly afraid in not doing it that he will be damned. Verily, the life of obedience unto the law is a life of defeat and frustration.

On the other hand, the life of grace in the Spirit of Christ liberates the man from the yoke and the bondage of dread and insecurity. The man finds peace in the goodness and the promise of God. What he does he does not out of fear and foreboding, but rather, his actions spring out of a full and grateful heart. The Gospel message is eminently correct in placing the motivation for living and for life in the Spirit, in the heart, in the inner man. Even the Scriptures themselves say that out of the heart flow the issues of life.

The Worst Sins Are the Sins of the Spirit

Our worst sins are always those in the heart, they are in the spirit. Cain slew his brother Abel because he was bitter in spirit, seeing that God refused his sacrifice and accepted the offering of Abel. Joseph's brethren hated him because they had no coat of many colors and they manifestly were not favorites of their father. Moses struck the rock in anger when God said, "Speak to it that the Lord might be honored." These bitternesses of spirit and these darknesses of heart pour bile and evil into the lifestream. Saul was eaten up of jealousy and envy when he heard the women of Israel singing, "Saul hath slain his thousands but David his tens of thousands." Elijah sat under a juniper tree wishing that he might die, depressed in spirit, because, running before the chariot of Ahab, he thought that on Mt. Carmel he had won the whole world to Jehovah. Nothing wears out the saints like running before the chariot of Ahab, persuaded that in our victories we have overcome carnal opposition. The spirit sinks in frustrations when we see the depths, heights, and strength of the foes who oppose us.

The unsympathetic and recalcitrant spirit leads us to undo the will of God. Jonah, refusing to go to Nineveh, hating those Gentile dogs, turned the opposite way to Tarsus, and when God did have mercy upon the repentant city, Jonah sat under a gourd vine praying that he might die. He was remonstrating with God for saving the lost! Judas, selling his Lord for thirty pieces of silver to placate his mercenary and covetous spirit, sought to retrieve what little he could from a lost cause, seeing that the Lord Jesus would certainly be delivered to the Romans. The elder brother, coming in from the fields, found that his younger brother had returned home. But instead of rejoicing, he pouted in anger and refused to enter the house.

When the father came out and entreated him saying, "Son, thou art ever with me," the boy replied, "At no time did I transgress thy commandment, but when this *thy son* (not my brother) who has wasted his life in harlotry and in riotous living, comes back home, for him you kill the fatted calf and the whole family makes merry." Heaven and earth instinctively dislike the attitude of the elder brother. The sins of the spirit are the worst sins of human life.

Triads of Blessings and Virtues

Out of the heart and out of the spirit are those issues that color, ultimately, finally, fundamentally, all living. That is why, I repeat, the Gospel places the motivation for the worship of God and the service of the Lord in the fullness of the heart, in the freeness of the spirit. "For the *karpos* (Greek singular), the effect, the produce, the result," the fruit of the Spirit is—then Paul names all these virtues listed in the text. You see, they are all one, they are all of the heart, they are all of an abounding soul. There is hardly ever just one grape, for grapes grow in clusters. Not just one of them ripens, they all ripen. So the produce of the spirit is a cluster. It is many and the many are one. A man will find in his own life, when he cultivates a good trait or virtue, that there will spring up around it a multitude of other blessed virtues. Thus it is with the *karpos* of the spirit.

In the text is named a triad of triads, three threes. The *karpos,* the result, the fruit, the produce, the effect of the spirit in the heart is "love, joy, peace." This describes our relationship to God; that is, not dreading to see Him, not walking before Him with foreboding, but in love, joy, and peace. It describes for the Christian a marvelous, open, free fellowship with God. The next triad is "longsuffering, gentleness, goodness." This is our relationship and our attitude toward those around us. We are not to be acrimonious and critical. Rather, we are to be "longsuffering, gentle, and good." The next triad refers to the Christian character that grows from within us, "faith, meekness, temperance." This inward responsiveness of the regenerated love has nothing to do with law. Law cannot create it. It comes from an overflowing spirit of love and gratitude to the Lord. This Pauline series of noble excellencies produced by the Spirit presents the Christian as one who has a relationship perpendicular to God and horizontal toward his brother man. The Christian lives in the fullness, the gladness, the victory, and the triumph of a wonderful and glorious spirit.

Love as a Fruit of the Spirit

For our continuing discussion we choose just one of the fruits of the spirit that is named here in the text. "For the *karpos* (the effect, the fruit, the produce, the result) of the Spirit (of a wonderful heart, of a new man in Christ) is *love. . . .*" Paul names "love, joy, peace, longsuffering, gentleness, goodness, faith, meekness, temperance," but we choose just one of them, "love." If the man is to live under law and if he gains his commendations before God by obedience to commandments and the observances of ceremonies and rituals, where would love ever have a place? Could law ever produce love by coercion? Make a man love? Law cannot do that, not as long as the man is created free. If the man is a robot, then God might command his heart and make him love the Lord. But if the man is free, God cannot coerce, command, mandate his love, for that has to be given away. It comes of a choice, of a free spirit, of a response in the soul. That alone is the foundation of love. If it is forced, if it is commanded, if it is mandated, if it is threatened, it is not love. For love is something born of the soul, something given away, something that arises out of a free spirit. The result of God's goodness to us in regenerating our souls, in the making of a new man and a new creation of us—the fruit of it, is an abounding and overflowing love.

You see, when a man begins thinking, "Oh, how good God is to me, sending Jesus to die for my sins, letting me call His name in prayer, bringing before Him all of my problems and burdens," then the man finds blessings with fresh remembrances of Gods' gifts every day. They are like manna, fresh every day. Truly, how wonderfully good God is to us! He has prepared for us a home in heaven. Our Savior has gone to open a door into glory and to make for us a mansion in the new city. Our Savior stands by us, comforts us, and strengthens us. He smooths our pillows on beds of affliction and encourages us in our hours of need. Out of the heart of gratitude, whether we are sick or whether we are well, come many sweet responses to God. They are not commanded, nor coerced, but they just rise out of the fullness of the heart. That is the response that God delights in from us.

Pleasing God With a Gift of Love

Are you not that way? Tell me, if you have a child, do you want him to obey you because if he does not you are going to beat him to death? And if you do not beat him to death, then he does not obey you? Is that the response you seek from the child? Rather, would you not like the child to do what he does in his spirit and in his attitude toward you because he loves you? I think God is that way. He does not want His children to serve Him and to walk in His presence in dread and fear like cringing slaves, as if God would beat them to death if they did not obey. No! What would please the Lord is that what we do, we do out of a fullness of heart, loving the Lord, desiring to do it. Is it not this in the Holy Scriptures that pleases God? "And Abel brought to the Lord a *minchah,*" sometimes in the Bible translated "offering." Another translation for *minchah* found in the Scriptures is "sacrifice." The word *minchah* is the ordinary Hebrew word for "gift." "And Abel brought of the firstlings of his flock a *minchah,* a gift, to the Lord." And the Lord looked into the heart of Abel and saw Abel's love for God and Abel's desire to show his affection, gratitude, and thanksgiving to God, and the Lord was pleased with Abel and his *minchah,* his gift.

Was not that the loving spirit of Hannah? She was persecuted by Peninnah. Her own soul was in distress because her womb was shut up and she had no child. She bowed her soul before the Lord and prayed and said that if God would look upon the low estate and the sorrow of His handmaiden and give her a child, she would give the lad to the Lord all the days of his life. And after little Samuel was laid in her bosom, when she weaned the child she brought him to old Eli, the pastor at the church in Shiloh, and gave a *minchah,* the gift of the boy to God. And the Lord was pleased with the gift and blessed the little boy and all Israel knew from Dan to Beersheba that he was sent to be a prophet in Israel. That feeling, that wanting, that desiring, that outflowing of the heart Godward pleases the Lord.

I remember reading a story in 2 Samuel. Bethlehem was in the hands of the uncircumcised, blaspheming, heathen Philistines. David was a hounded, hunted refugee. At that time David exclaimed, "Oh, for a drink of water from the well which is by the gate of Bethlehem." And two of David's mighty men, Abishai and Ittai, heard David say that, and so great was their love for their leader that they braved the lines of the Philistines and drew a draft of water from the well at the gate of Bethlehem and brought it to David, a *minchah,* a gift of love. David, seeing those men jeopardizing their lives just for him said, "I cannot drink it." And he poured the water out, a libation before God. Think of that *minchah!* It was the expression of devotion on the part of those warriors to their chief, David.

Is that not what moved the Lord in Bethany, when Mary took an alabaster box of ointment of spikenard and broke it over His head and anointed the Lord and the perfume filled the place? Such an act of love and affection and gratitude! But some of those carping critics who were present said: "Look at that waste! It could have been sold for three hundred pence (a year's salary), and given to the poor." But the Lord said: "Let her alone. Wherever this gospel is preached there will this be spoken of what she has done for me." The extravagance of the gift, the *minchah!* Yet it pleased and honored the Lord. Out of the fullness of the soul, out of an abounding heart of love and gratitude, Mary poured out the perfume, the ointment, the spikenard, upon the blessed Savior.

This love is to be the motivation of our lives. This is the *karpos,* the fruit, the effect, the produce, the result, of the new spirit we have. Not serving God like a galley slave, not like a penitentiary inmate before his warden, not like a cringing servant before his master, but serving God out of the fullness of the heart. The born-again Christian says, "This I would like to say to God, this I would like to do for God, this would I like to give to God, because I love the Lord with all my soul." His faithful worship arises not out of obedience to commandments, mandates, and laws, but out of a heart of love.

Was it not so when the Lord sat over against the treasury

and watched the people as they placed gifts and tithes into the treasury? A poor widow came by who cast into the treasury all that she had, just trusting God for daily bread. Was there any commandment that she do that? No! What was it that pleased God and made Jesus notice her as He watched the people? It was the fullness of her heart and her gratitude thus expressed when she gave into the treasury of the Lord everything that she had. This was her *minchah,* her gift. She did it out of praise, appreciation, and gratitude for the goodness of God.

Worshiping God Out of the Fullness of the Heart

John, the sainted apostle, was by himself on the lonely, stony isle of Patmos, there sentenced to die of exposure and possible starvation. On the Lord's day, the day of the week when Jesus was raised from the dead, John was in the Spirit. Is there any commandment for us to worship God and assemble on the Lord's Day? No. There is not a syllable in the Bible commanding us to do this. Why, then, is John in the spirit of praise, and worship, and communion on the Lord's Day? It was an observance that arose out of the fullness of His heart. The disciples thus honored and worshiped Christ from the beginning. There is no commandment to observe any Sunday, any Lord's Day. There is a commandment for Israel to keep the Sabbath Day. On the Sabbath Day they are under commandment to offer two lambs. They are under commandment, if someone picks up sticks on the Sabbath Day, to stone the transgressor to death. They are under commandment not to light a fire on the Sabbath Day and to observe a thousand other rules. But what is this we do on the Lord's Day? We worship the Lord, not out of commandment, but out of the love, praise, and gratitude that we feel in our hearts. When the Lord was raised from the dead, the disciples, out of the love for the living Jesus, gathered together on the day of His resurrection, the first day of the week, and sang songs, prayed prayers, taught the people, and blessed God. Because they were commanded to do it? No. They did it because they had it in their hearts to do it. It came out of the fullness of their spirits. And that is the way we ought to be about our service before God. We are absolutely free from the mandates and commandments of the law. They have no more pertinency for us. They are nailed to the cross with all the ordinances of the Old Covenant.

Well then, how do you feel, now that you are free? Do you feel like going out and blaspheming the name of God and forgetting the Lord and living a life of selfishness, iniquity, and violence? No! It is the opposite. When I call to mind what the Lord has done for me in order that He might save me from the judgment and penalty of my sins, and when I remember the promises of God for me now and in the world to come, Lord, Lord, to bow in Thy presence is a sweet privilege. To sing songs of praise and glory is a gladness and a benediction to my soul. To gather with God's people in God's house is a sweet fellowship, like the ointment that fell from Aaron's beard in Psalm 133. Oh, the sweet fellowship of God's people! I want to come to church. "I was glad when they said unto me, Let us go up to the house of the Lord." This is the true motivation of the Christian life, worshiping God not out of coercion and not out of commandment, not out of fear and dread lest we be damned if we do it not, but we are doing what we do for God out of the fullness of the heart. This I want to do, to bring a *minchah* to the Lord as a sign that I love Him, to offer the praise, the sacrifice of my lips in honor and in gratitude for the Lord. Such worship is a high and holy privilege. A thousand other things we do for God, not because we have to, but because it is in our hearts thus to respond. This is the fruit, the effect, of the Spirit in our lives.

Chapter 19

FALLING IN A FAULT

> Brethren, if a man be overtaken in a fault, ye which are spiritual, restore such an one in the spirit of meekness; considering thyself, lest thou also be tempted.
>
> Bear ye one another's burdens, and so fulfil the law of Christ. (Gal. 6:1, 2)

We now come to an exposition of Galatians 6:1. It reads as follows: "Brethren, if a man be overtaken in a *paraptoma* [if a man be overtaken in a falling away, in a falling aside, in a fault], ye which are spiritual [*hoi pneumatikoi,* the spiritual people of the Lord], restore such an one in the spirit of meekness; considering thyself, lest thou also be *peirasthes,* tempted, tried." We are to consider especially this part of the text: "Brethren, if a man be overtaken in a *paraptoma,* a falling away, a turning aside, a fault."

How unusual that Paul should address these words to the Christians of Galatia! Had they not been born again? Yes. Had they not been regenerated? Yes. Had they not become partakers of the divine nature? Yes. Was there not emplanted in their hearts the incorruptible Word of God? Yes. Did not the Holy Spirit dwell in their souls? Yes. Then how is it that he speaks of a man here as being overtaken in a fault? Surely a regenerated, saved, Christian man would not fall into a *paraptoma.* But he does, for I find in my own self, in my own experience, in the churches I have pastored, and in the Scriptures themselves that one of the things that characterizes God's people is *paraptoma,* fault. Human fault and failure are universal; the experience is not unique or separate or peculiar. It characterizes all of us. "If a man be overtaken in a fault. . . ."

Look at the youngsters who are growing up in our homes. When these children are saved they are converted, they are born again, they are young Christians, but, oh, how much they have yet to learn, and how many mistakes will they yet make, and how many faults, mistakes, failures, and shortcomings will they know even in their young lives! These teenagers are saved, they have been regenerated, they have been baptized. Many of them have consecrated their lives in full commitment to the Lord, but, oh, the days of trials that they face and in how many instances will they find failures a concomitant of their Christian life. Even those of us who are grown and mature in the Lord, we who have been saved, regenerated, and baptized, we who belong to the household of faith and have been down this pilgrimage road for years and years, even we find ourselves in fault, in shortcoming.

Faults and Failures in the Best of God's People

James and John, the sons of Zebedee, were at the very heart of the ministry of our Savior. They belonged to the Lord's inner circle. At the Last Supper John leaned his head against the bosom of Christ and Simon Peter, sitting next to John, asked him to ask Jesus who it was that should betray Him. James and John were so close to Jesus, yet it was that pair of brothers who came to the Lord with a most selfish request. They were encouraged and directed by their own mother to say to the Lord Jesus: "We do not know about these other disciples, they can find their places as they may, but as for us, put one of us on Your right hand and put the other of us on Your left hand. Make one of us Prime Minister in the kingdom and the other of us Chancellor of the Exchequer. As for the rest of the disciples, let them find their rightful place down at the foot of the ladder." That is James and John.

Simon Peter was the chief of the apostles. He was the one whom God chose to bring to the Jews, to the Samaritans, and to the Gentiles the open door of faith and the receiving of the Holy Spirit. When the Lord said, "All of you will forsake me this night," Simon Peter avowed, "Lord, all of these other disciples may forsake Thee, but *I, I* would never forsake Thee;

I would die for Thee." And the Lord replied: "Simon, would you die for Me? Truly, truly, I say to you, before the cock crows twice, [the cock crows at midnight and at dawn], before the morning comes, you shall thrice deny that you even know Me." It was this same Simon Peter after Pentecost, after Samaria, after Caesarea, and after the glorious years of his early ministry, who came to Antioch and there played the hypocrite before the church of the Lord. The Apostle Paul accosted him and told him to his face that he was to be condemned because of his dissimulation. Simon Peter, of all men! "Brethren, if a man be overtaken in a fault. . . ." If I know of anything that characterizes us, it is *paraptoma*. All of us.

Extremities of Attitudes Toward Human Weaknesses

Now the attitude toward failure and human weakness among men oscillates between extremities. For example, the organized church in the earth is sometimes most severe and Puritanical, then again it can be most permissive, very much so. Let us examine the church as I have seen it in my own lifetime. When I was a boy I grew up in a small congregation in a little town. There was a somewhat affluent man who belonged to the church. All of us were as poor as Job's turkeys but he was just one notch above the poverty of the rest of us, so he shined. He was the president of our little state bank in the town, a bank that later went bankrupt and defunct. He dressed nattily and spoke like a cultured man. One day they hailed him before the church and accused him of dancing. The church was called into council. You never saw such a dog fight in your life. This man went up to the preacher and slapped him in the face. There I was, a little boy sitting in the church and looking at all that was going on, all that acrimonious castigation. They turned the banker out of the church for dancing. It tore that little church to shreds. Now, I am not saying here whether they should have turned him out or not, but I surely can tell you how I felt about it as a little boy. As I sat there in the church and listened to the people of the church bring charges against the banker for dancing and all the things that they said to him about him, and all that went on in that session, then finally voted to turn him out, I saw the sad repercussion in the hearts of the people. The tragedy made an indelible impression upon me.

What of the church to which I now belong? I could not conceive of that today. It would be unspeakable to me that this church would be called into business session and we would give ourselves to slapping the pastor and to acrimonious castigation, turning one another out. When I looked at it as a boy I thought those that turned him out were no better than the one they turned out. Maybe he should have turned them out! "Brethren, if a man be overtaken in a *paraptoma,* a fault. . . ."

If such differing attitudes characterize the church, think how the world oscillates! It goes from one extremity to the other. In the days of the cavaliers under Charles I there was a permissive society in England. Then the pendulum swung the other direction and they took Charles I and cut off his head. Oliver Cromwell, the Puritan, came to head the Commonwealth. In those days pleasure of any kind was looked upon with disdain. I read in a history where a historical wag said that the Commonwealth was against bear baiting, not because they were particularly compassionate for the bear but because they did not like the pleasure it brought to the bear hunters. After the Commonwealth the people brought Charles II to the throne and the Cavaliers were back again. Thus does human society oscillate from one extremity to the other.

If that differing attitude toward fault is true in society and government, think how true it is in our individual lives. Look at how we are. Here is an affluent man, successful and famous. But he also has faults, derelictions, sins, and failures. Because of his position and his wealth we have a tendency to overlook his sin and to look upon them as eccentricities and idiosyncracies. But if the fellow is ragged and poor and he falls into faults and failures, he brings down the wrath of society on his defenseless head. I am just telling you how we in the world react toward fault, failure, sin, and shortcomings.

The Scriptural Attitude of Love and Mercy

Now may I point out to you that there is no finer evidence of the inspiration of the Holy Scriptures to be found than in its attitude toward human weakness. The basic ground from which the Holy Scriptures look upon sin, fault, and failure never changes. The Bible never retreats, it never retracts, it never withdraws. It is ever stern and impersonal. It is no respecter of persons. The law is applied impersonally and inexorably. "The soul that sins shall die." "The wages of sin is death." And the pastor of the church in Jerusalem in James 2:10 wrote, "For whosoever shall keep the whole law, and yet offend in one point, he is guilty of all." It is as though he has broken all of the commandments. He is a sinner, and the wages of sin is death. That is the law, and the law never changes, it never retreats, and it never retracts. In the judgmental level it looks upon mankind in stern reality and in awesome condemnation. And it never changes.

But that is what Galatians is all about, and that is what the Gospel is all about. There is freedom of deliverance in Christ. The law condemns us because of our faults and our failures, our sins and our shortcomings. Against the white light of God's pure holiness we are black. The law slays us. But this is the Gospel, the good news, the evangel; namely, in Christ Jesus we have full forgiveness. What the law could not do in that it was weak through the flesh, and what we could not do because we are born in sin and conceived in iniquity, the Gospel of Christ, the mercy of God, the goodness of God, the forebearance and compassion and forgiveness of God did for us. God reached down through Jesus Christ and saved us. The Apostle John wrote it so beautifully, "For if the law came by Moses [if death and judgment and condemnation came by the Ten Commandments], then grace and truth came by Jesus Christ." If a man was bitten by the snake of sin, God's provision of salvation was so simple and so merciful he had but to look to live. The loving purpose of God is not to damn but to save. John wrote, "For God sent not his Son into the world to condemn the world but that the world through him might be saved" (John 3:17).

> He did not come to condemn the world,
> He did not come to blame.
> He did not come only to seek,
> It was to save that He came.
> And when we call Him "Jesus," Saviour,
> We call Him by His name.

Paul wrote in Romans 6:23, "The wages of sin is death [yes, how tragically true!]; but the gift of God is eternal life through Jesus Christ our Lord [How triumphantly victorious!]." This is Paul's message for us who have looked in faith to Jesus.

The Loving Spirit of the True Christian

"Brethren, if a man be overtaken in a *paraptoma,* a falling away, a turning aside, a fall; if a man be overtaken in a fault, *hoi kneumatikoi,* you who love Jesus, restore such a one in the spirit of meekness; considering thyself, lest thou also be *pierasthes,* tempted, tried yourself." What a difference in spirit and attitude ought to be found in the household of faith from that found in the unbelieving world. But just the opposite is so often true. It is the church that is hypercritical and full of condemnation. I have often thought that if I ever fell into a fault, into a *paraptoma,* O God, do not let me fall into the hands of those censorious, cirtical judges in the church. Let me fall into the hands of the barkeepers, the streetwalkers, the dope peddlers, and the pushers. Why? Because so often church people would tear me apart with their long, wagging, gossipy tongues, cutting me to shreds. They would stand as self-appointed censors and judges and crush the spirit and the life out of me. Is not that true? But really and actually, the censorious hypocrites in the church are but caricatures of the real thing. They are the Pharisees of this generation who lift themselves up as being superior to these who have fallen around them and they say, "Lord, I thank Thee that I am not like other men and especially not like those sinners over there." Is that the loving spirit of God? Is that the spirit that should characterize the people of Christ? "Brethren, if a man be overtaken in a *paraptoma, hoi pneumatikoi,* you who love Jesus restore such a one in the spirit of meekness, looking at yourself, lest thou also be tried." My brother, there is not a sin in the category of which we are not capable of committing. I am including murder. There is not a man but who is capable of murder. Practically every murderer to be found in the penitentiary became so in a moment of wrath and violent reaction. You are capable of that, too. "Lest you yourself, *peirathes,* be tried."

What then is the spirit of the Christian, of the born-again

believer, toward human weakness, fault, and failure? Our attitude is to be one that reflects the mind and heart of Christ. We are not in the judging business. That is God's business. We are not in the condemning business, that is God's business. "Vengeance belongeth unto me, I will recompense, saith the Lord. And again, The Lord shall judge his people" (Heb. 10:30). That is God's business. Our business is the healing business, the helping business, the forgiving business, the encouraging business, that is our business, that is our mandate and assignment from heaven.

One time in the Bible James and John came to the Lord Jesus and said: "Lord Jesus, we announced in that Samaritan village over yonder that You were coming and they rejected the announcement. They will not let You into the city gates. You are unwelcome." Then James and John added, "Now Lord, bid us to call fire down from God out of heaven, and burn them up, burn them up as Elijah did." But the Lord turned and rebuked them and said, "Ye know not what manner of spirit ye are of. For the Son of man is not come to destroy men's lives, but to save them . . ." (Luke 9:55, 56). We are not in the judging business, and we are not in the condemning business. We are not in the censorious business, we are not in the castigating business—that is God's business. Our business is to help, to pray, to love, to encourage, to be merciful, to be compassionate. "If a man be overtaken in a fault, restore him." Pray, love, help, lift him up. That is our business. That is our calling.

I remember driving down to my little rural church in Kentucky. On the way down the Dixie Highway a big new car passed me at a high rate of speed. When I reached the little community I turned from the highway and followed the road for a mile or so. Where the road made a right angle turn there was a high, dirt embankment with a farmer's house on the top of it. By the time I drove to that corner, to my sorrow I saw that big beautiful car a wreck. It had plowed into the embankment, going so fast that the driver could not negotiate the right turn. It was a shambles of a car; it really hit the embankment. By the time I could get there, the farmer and his dear wife were helping the injured man out of the car. He apparently had gone through the glass windshield and had been cut to pieces, for he was covered with blood. The farmer was on one side of him and his wife was on the other side of him and they were helping him to the farm home to care for and to minister to him. I presume it would have been legalistically possible for me to stand before the man and say: "Do not drive so fast. Do you not know that you cannot negotiate these turns at such a terrific speed? Do you not know better than to break the law and the speed limits?" And on and on. How much better for us to be like that compassionate farmer who took the hurt man out from behind the wheel. That is our business. That is our assignment: to help. And if I cannot help, then I can pray. My business is not condemning others in a censorious, judgmental attitude. That belongs to God. My business is to love, to help, to pray, to forgive, to encourage, and to respond in compassion.

"Brethren, if a man be overtaken in a fault, ye who are spiritual restore such a one in the spirit of meekness, considering thyself, lest thou also be *peirasthes,* lest thou also be tempted, fall into a fault." Not one of us is above that falling. "Let him that thinketh he standeth take heed lest he fall" (1 Cor. 10:12). And what you point in someone else is doubtless the weakness in your own life. That is why you notice it. That is why you talk about it. That is why you gossip about it. "Lest thou also be tried, *peirasthes,* tempted."

In the days gone by in Great Britain there was a flaming preacher by the name of John Bradford. He lived in the days of Cranmer, Ridley, and Latimer. He preached out on the Commons, outside where the people were, proclaiming the good news of the grace of God in Christ Jesus. (By the way, when Mary Tudor, "Bloody Mary," came to the throne, she burned John Bradford at Smithfield, England, at the stake. She burned Latimer, Ridley, Cranmer, and three hundred other of the great ministers of Christ.) One day John Bradford was out on the Commons, preaching to a throng of villagers about the goodness of God and the saving knowledge of Jesus. He was standing on a box or a stone, preaching his heart out. While he was preaching, at the edge of the crowd the sheriff and the bailiff and their henchmen passed by escorting a man who had a rope around his neck. The poor fellow was to be hanged. In the middle of his sermon John Bradford stopped preaching and with his eye he followed the sheriff and the bailiff and the henchmen leading that man with the rope around his neck. Then John Bradford, the preacher of Jesus, lifted up his right hand, pointed to the sheriff, and said, "My brethren, there but for the grace of God go I." Why is it that we have not fallen into some of the unthinkable sorrows and heartaches that we find afflicting others? It is not because we are any better, though we think we are. It is not because we are superior, though we suppose we are. It is not because they are the dregs of the earth and we are the angelic elect of heaven. It is not because we are any better; it is only because God has grace and mercy upon us. He somehow chose in His sovereign grace to be good to us. Why was I not born a heathen Hottentot, living in ignorance and darkness and superstition? I am a Christian American only because God was good to me. That is why it behooves us who name the name of Jesus always to be humble in His presence and compassionate, understanding, and sympathetic in our attitude toward others. If I can help, I want to try. If I cannot help, then I will just pray. But, O God, seal my lips from censorious judgment and hurtful criticism. Oh, do not you wish the whole church was like that? The very spire on it is a symbol of our faith, pointing men toward God. We are all sinners alike, saved by the mercy of God. There is no limit to the heights and depths of the love and the grace of God in Christ Jesus, and it reaches even to me.

Chapter 20

SOWING AND REAPING

> Be not deceived; God is not mocked: for whatsoever a man soweth, that shall he also reap.
>
> For he that soweth to his flesh shall of the flesh reap corruption; but he that soweth to the Spirit shall of the Spirit reap life everlasting.
>
> And let us not be weary in well-doing: for in due season we shall reap, if we faint not.
>
> As we have therefore opportunity, let us do good unto all men, especially unto them who are of the household of faith. (Gal. 6:7-10)

In our study of the Book of Galatians we are in the middle of chapter 6 and the reading of the text begins at verse 9 and concludes at verse 10: "Let him that is taught in the word communicate unto him that teacheth in all good things. Be not deceived; God is not mocked: for whatsoever a man soweth, that shall he also reap. For he that soweth to his flesh shall of the flesh reap corruption; but he that soweth to the Spirit shall of the Spirit reap life everlasting. And let us not be weary in well-doing: for in due season we shall reap, if we faint not." We have heard that passage quoted about sowing and reaping all our lives. Since this is an exposition we present it in its context, even as Paul gave it meaning in the inspiration of God.

What Paul is talking about is supporting the ministry, giving to the church. "Let him that is taught in the Word" (let the congregation of the Lord), "communicate unto him that teacheth us" (supporting the church, supporting the ministry). The word translated "communicate" is a Pauline expression used several times in his letters by which he referred to liberality, to giving. The Greek word is *koinoneo,* to participate, to share. *Koinonia* is a sharing. Sometimes it is translated "a fellowship." Sometimes it is translated "a communion." *Koinonikos* is the word for liberal; someone who is *koinonikos* is liberal. A *koinonos* is a partner, a sharer. What the apostle is writing to churches at Galatia is that those who belong to the church and are blessed by the Word of God are to share what they have with those who teach the way of the Lord. Let them be liberal in their response. Let them support the ministry graciously. Then Paul writes a word of universal law, "For whatsoever a man soweth" [talking about his giving] "that shall be also reap" [talking about the harvest that comes from it]. "For he that soweth to his flesh shall of the fleshly world reap its disintegration, its corruption, but the that soweth the spiritual things of God shall of the spiritual world reap life in heavenly degree." The Apostle then adds: "Do not let us be weary in this ministry for in due season we shall certainly reap through the law of the harvest. Let us not faint or be weary in it."

The Same Laws in the Spiritual as in the Natural World

An objector can say: "The law of sowing and reaping is certainly true in the physical, mundane, terrestrial world, but it is not applicable in the spiritual world." Just the opposite is true. I could not think of a finer argument for the Creator of things visible and invisible, of things spiritual and physical, than what we see and what we experience in this unified workmanship of God. His laws are the same in the unseen world as here in the seen world. The same plan, the same design, the same intelligence, runs through all of it—the natural and the supernatural, the spiritual and the physical.

The Lord God, when He laid down the plan for the creation of His physical universe, followed the same law, the same plan, and the same design as had been in existence ever since God Himself existed, which is from eternity. Everywhere we see evidences of the same workmanship, the same mind, the same God. What we find in the spiritual world is the same kind of wheels of genius and wisdom that we find in the physical world, only in the spiritual world the workmanship is without clothing or substance. I used to say there are two great books that God has written. He has written a book that we call the natural world and we see the hand of God in it. Then He has written a book called the spiritual world, and we see the hand of God in that. Having thought of that more carefully, I have come to the conclusion that there is one book, just one, written by the finger and hand of God, and its two chapters are separated only by the narrow demarcation of our five senses. Whether it is natural or supernatural, visible or invisible, whether it is spiritual or natural, it is the same.

Wherever you touch God's work, when you get beyond the rudiments, beyond the primaries, there you will bump into everything else that God has done. It is one system, built on one plan, guided by one intelligence, and laid down according to one purpose. For example, suppose a man gives himself to the study of agronomy, agriculture. It is not long until he is in botany, the study of plant life. It is not long until he is in zoology, the study of animal life. It is not long until he is in the study of meteorology, the atmosphere, the moisture, the rain. As he studies agronomy, he is beginning to bump into everything else that God has done. There is no exception to that in the study of anything where we look at the workmanship of Almighty God. It is one universe, one world, one law, one great design, one mighty intelligence, one Lord God who has wrought it all.

So the laws that we see in the physical world are the same laws that we meet in the spiritual world and one of them Paul refers to here—the law of sowing and reaping. Our Lord, the Master-Teacher, saw that clearly. Observing the connection of things, the interrelatedness of things, He would take a spiritual idea and illustrate it by what he saw in humble, physical life. In seeing a bird fly, or one that fell to the ground, or in seeing the wild flowers grow, the lilies of the field, He would see merciful evidence of the watchful, guardian care of almighty God. Paul followed the Lord Jesus in that way of teaching, and a truly fine minister will employ that same technique today. The language that he uses may be very simple, rural in fact, such as sowing and reaping, but what he is actually talking about is the mighty law of compensation, or the law of retribution, or the law of cause and effect. The law is the same whether visible or invisible. So the Apostle Paul speaking of us and what we do in our lives, what we give ourselves to, what we love, what we do with our hands, and what desires fill our hearts, uses a plain, simple, natural law to illustrate the spiritual law of sowing and reaping, planting and harvesting. Paul speaks of this law in two ways, one, in kind and the other in degree.

The Law of Sowing and Reaping in Kind

First, the law of sowing and reaping in kind. "Whatsoever a man soweth *that* shall he also reap," not something else, but *that*. "Whatsoever a man soweth, *that* shall he reap." Anything for sale, and you pay a price for it, you buy *that*, whatever it is. For the student, it is knowledge; for the soldier, it could be fame; for the workman, it is money, compensation; but whatever one buys he pays the price for *that*. So it is in our planting and harvesting. Whatever we sow, we reap *that*. A man would be surprised if his harvest were something else and different. If he sows wheat he does not expect sorghum. If he plants an acorn, he does not expect a magnolia. If he plants a slip of a little elm, he expects a great big elm tree some day. What a man sows, *that* does he reap. Here is a young man who goes to school to be trained in the field of medicine. Therefore, he is not expected to be a skillful farmer because he is trained in medicine. Or a young man goes to school and is taught law, therefore, he is not expected to be a skillful engineer. What he sows he reaps. What he gives his life to, the harvest is *that*.

So it is in the spiritual world, the apostle avows. What a man sows, that does he reap. And if he sows to the world, if he sows to the flesh, if the energy and the outreach of his life is for things mundane, terrestrial, fleshly, carnal, worldly, then the harvest ultimately is inevitable decay, loss, and corruption.

Actually, that is an astonishing truth. When a man gives himself to the world and he sows to the flesh, his harvest can be money, affluence, success, pleasure, freedom from hunger, cold, and heat. In how many ways can he find a harvest sowing to the flesh, sowing to the world, a harvest that is seemingly grand. But the apostle says there is also another harvest in it and that harvest is corruption, decay, loss. The apostle says that there are no spiritual rewards, there are no spiritual harvests, when a man sows just to the world. For example, money can buy a bed but not sleep. Money can buy food but not appetite. Money can buy a house but not a home. Money can buy medicine but not health. Money can buy amusement and pleasure but not happiness. Money can buy gifts but not love. Money can buy a crucifix but not a Savior. When we sow to the flesh, to the world, when our vision and dream are down here terrestrial, carnal, fleshly, then the harvest is corruption, loss and decay.

One time two men were driving through a beautiful estate crowned by a lovely mansion with fertile fields all around it. The man asked his companion, "What is the value of this great estate?" His friend replied, "I cannot tell you the value of it but I can tell you what it cost the owner." The other fellow said "What?" And he replied: "It cost him everything that he had. It cost him his soul."

The Vicar of a church, an Anglican church in England, was kneeling by the side of one of his wealthy parishioners and was pleading with the man to give his heart to God. The minister said to him, "Sir, if you will give your life to God, your soul to God, your heart to God, take my hand." But the man refused. Then the Vicar pled with him: "Sir, the end is drawing near. Life is fleeting. Death is nigh. Give your heart to God. Take my hand." But again the man refused. When he died his cold, pulseless hand relaxed and in it the pastor saw the key to his safe, as though he could take his possessions with him. "He that soweth to the flesh shall of the flesh reap corruption."

Men initiated into a certain fraternal order could never forget one of the most dramatic parts of the instruction. The architect is slain and his friend seeks to raise him from the dead. He takes his cold, dead, corrupting hand and seeks to raise him up. But the friend turns and says: "I cannot raise him. I cannot lift him, for the skin slips from his corrupting hand."

There was a wealthy man who had given his life to the

world and not to God. In his last illness he became obsessed with his hands. His wife called his partner in business in order that he come and talk to John. "Maybe you can help him," she said, "he is obsessed with his hands." So Jim came to see his old friend whom he had known and loved through the years. As he visited by his side, Jim finally said to him, "John, there is nothing wrong with your hands." But John looked at him and said: "Jim, look! My God, Jim, they are so empty! They are so empty!" He that soweth to the flesh, to the world, shall of the flesh reap emptiness, corruption, decay, and loss. Death, inexorable, inevitable death comes to the one who sows to the flesh, who sows to the world. Death becomes to the lost man a mockery, a ghastly, ghostly, apparition. Death to the lost man is not the gate to glory. He that soweth to the flesh shall of the flesh reap corruption, loss, disintegration. He reaps in kind.

The Law of Sowing and Reaping in Degree

We now discuss sowing and harvesting in degree. "Let him that is taught, those who belong to the congregation of the Lord, *koinoneo,* share, contribute, support him that teacheth" [the church, the ministry,] "for he that soweth in the spirit of God, in the things of God, supporting the work of God, shall of that same God reap a harvest in greater degree, elevated, multiplied." Ah, Paul wrote so much about that. He writes in 2 Corinthians 9: "But this I say, He which soweth sparingly shall reap also sparingly; and he which soweth bountifully shall reap also bountifully. Every man according as he purposeth in his heart, so let him give; not grudgingly [not under coercion, not by force,]; or of necessity: for God loveth a cheerful giver" (vv. 6,7). A man who loves the work of the Lord and supports it triumphantly, gloriously, liberally, for that man God is able to make all grace abound toward him in highest degree (2 Cor. 9:8). Sowing in the name of God, in the work of the Lord, but the harvest—O dear Lord, how full and how rich, how blessed, how precious, how triumphant! The law of the spiritual harvest brings spiritual reward, spiritual blessings. Sowing and reaping, planting and harvesting.

Many times people ask me, "Did you ever know Dr. Truett?"

(He was pastor of the First Baptist Church, Dallas, for forty-seven years.) I reply: "I never knew him as a pastor or someone that I had seen frequently or intimately. I just knew him from afar. I would go to a Southern Baptist Convention or a great convocation and listen to him." But the effect he had upon me as upon everyone else was sometimes almost indescribable. Here is an instance. At one of our conventions, he was describing his preaching to the cowboys in West Texas. Every summer he would go out there and preach to those cowmen. One day after a morning service one of those ranchers who had vast acres and herds said, "Dr. Truett, would you walk with me?" So the pastor and the cattleman walked and walked until finally they came to a lonely, isolated place. The cowman stopped and turned to the pastor and said, "Sir, today I have come to realize that these hundreds of thousands of acres of ranchland are not mine. They belong to God and I am but His steward. For the first time today I have come to see that these herds of cattle are not mine. They belong to God and I am just His steward. All these vast possessions that are supposed to be in my name are not mine at all. They belong to God, and I am to use them for His good and glory." He said: "Dr. Truett, I want you to kneel down here and I will kneel by your side and I want you to tell God for me that today I give Him all of my land, all of my herds, all of my cattle, and all of my possessions and that I will try to be a good steward, using them for the glory of God. You tell God that for me." So they knelt down and the great pastor with bowed head and humble heart by the side of that big cattleman dedicated to God everything that the man owned with the promise that he would use it for the glory of the Lord. In describing it Dr. Truett said he supposed that was all. It was a prayer of consecration and dedication of what the man possessed and he, God's steward, promised to use it wisely and well. But when Dr. Truett got through praying the cowman was not done. When the pastor finished the prayer of dedication the rancher put his hand on his arm and said: "Now, Dr. Truett, having given God everything that I have and having promised God that I would use it for His glory, now Dr. Truett, may I also give to God my wayward and prodigal boy? And may I ask God to save and bring back that wayward, prodigal child? Would you ask that from the Lord? Would you pray that to God?"

Oh, I not only found myself melted in tears, but I saw for the first time the truth of how God's blessings can come upon us. We have a right to ask a harvest in the spirit, having dedicated to God everything in the flesh, having consecrated to Him all we have in the world. We have a right to ask of God a blessing, and according to the immutable, inexorable laws of the Almighty, the harvest is certain. When I sow in the spirit, when I sow in prayer, when I sow in dedication, I have a right to expect in kind and in degree a harvest from His gracious hands.

Therefore, the apostle makes the appeal, "Let us not be weary, do not quit praying, do not be discouraged, do not be downcast, never, for in due season, in God's time, we shall reap." Sowing and reaping. Dedicating to God the love of our hearts, and the commitment of our souls, we can expect by the promise of God Himself answer to our prayers. Grace for grace, blessings a hundred fold, that is God. That is the Lord who made us and the universe in which we live. Ah, what more precious blessedness, what more tender, gracious sweetness than to give to God the issue of our lives, the dreams of our hearts, the prayers of our souls and then expect from God, never to be disappointed, the harvest of His rich grace and loving presence!

Chapter 21

THE GLORY OF THE CROSS

> But God forbid that I should glory, save in the cross of our Lord Jesus Christ, by whom the world is crucified unto me, and I unto the world. (Gal. 6:14)

Let us now begin with Galatians 6:11: "Ye see how large a letter I have written unto you with mine own hand. As many as desire to make a fair shew in the flesh, they constrain you to be circumcised; only lest they should suffer persecution for the cross of Christ. For neither they themselves who are circumcised keep the law; but desire to have you circumcised, that they may glory in your flesh. But God forbid that I should glory, save in the cross of our Lord Jesus Christ, by whom the world is crucified unto me, and I unto the world" (Gal. 6:11-14).

In the text Paul makes a contrast between the Galatians who glory in the flesh (the Greek word is *kauchaomai,* "glory," "boast,") and his own humble, committed spirit that forbids that he should glory, save in the cross of Jesus Christ. The Galatians in their propensity and affinity for glorying in the flesh, for turning aside from the salvation provided by the love and mercy of God in Jesus, and for turning to sophisticated human teachers, thought that in self-righteousness and self-commendation they should save themselves before God.

In the third chapter of this book Paul addressed them, "O foolish Galatians, who hath bewitched you?" (v. 1a). I think that if we were to take the letter and the appeal of the apostle written in the first century and apply it today he would have said, "O foolish modernists, who has bewitched you that you should glory in the flesh, in human effort, in human speculation? But God forbid that I should glory save in the cross of our Lord Jesus Christ." The cross with all of its naked hideousness, as the Roman would have it; the cross with all of its philosophical irrationality, as the Greek would have it; the cross with all of its shame and suffering, as the scribe would have it; but the cross with all of its love and mercy and forgiveness, as Paul preached it.

> In the cross of Christ I glory,
> Towering o'er the wrecks of time;
> All the light of sacred story
> Gathers round its head sublime.

"God forbid that I should glory, save in the cross of our Lord Jesus Christ."

The Sign of the Cross as an Emblem of the Christian Faith

The cross is a sign, an aegis, an emblem of the Christian faith. The whole course of history turned in A.D. 300 when Constantine was converted. In the midst of a battle for the throne of the Caesars Constantine said, "At midday I saw a sign in the sky, a cross, and underneath these words: '*In hoc signo vinces,*' 'in this sign conquer'." Upon this occasion, as upon countless other occasions before, the sign of the Gospel of the Son of God is found in a cross.

The insignia of the Christian faith is not two tables of stone containing the commandments of God. It is not a sword, a scimitar, a star, or a galaxy. The insignia of the Christian faith is not a seven-branched lampstand or even a halo above a submissive head. Rather, the insignia of the Christian faith is a stark, rude, crude, rugged cross.

Sometimes visiting the Roman Colosseum I stand and look at what is the best example of the cross that I know. Unlike what we think of as a decoration on the top of a church or as an ornament to wear around our necks made of gold and silver and studded with precious stones, the cross in the Colosseum is as rugged a crossbeam as could be ingeniously devised. I am told that it was placed there many years ago in honor and in memory of the early Christians who lost their lives in that terrible arena.

The cross speaks a universal language. All men everywhere understand it. Some time ago I sat in a great throng against the background of a mountain of Bavaria, listening to the Passion Play in Oberammergau. The thousands of people in attendance were from every nationality, tongue, tribe, family, and language under the sun. The play was in German and there were many of us who could not follow it in the Germanic tongue. But I had the unusual and deep persuasion that as we sat there and watched the drama of the suffering and crucifixion of our Lord, every man in his own language and in his own tongue understood it. The cross speaks to human hearts everywhere in every nation, in every language, in every family, clan, and tribe under God's heaven.

The cross of Christ is not a mythical, romantic idea, symbol, or story. It is historical and factual. If we think of the reference to Christ in Josephus as an interpolation, there are just two early first-century references to the Lord Jesus. They are found in Suetonius and Tacitus, Latin historians, and in both instances they refer to the crucifixion of our Lord. The historical reference was occasioned by the burning of Rome. When the people began to point their fingers at Nero as having done it, in order to obviate the suspicion, he said the Christians did it. Now that necessitated the early Roman historian to describe who the Christians were, for it was a strange, unusual, and unknown sect. So both Suetonius and Tacitus say that the Christians were followers of a felon who was crucified in Judaea under Pontius Pilate.

The cross is the cruelest instrument of execution that the human mind has ever devised. No Roman citizen could be crucified. Death by crucifixion was reserved for felons, insurrectionists, criminals, and murderers. It was especially opprobrious to the Jews. The Apostle Paul in Galatians 3 quoting Deuteronomy 21, quotes Moses as saying, "Cursed is everyone who is hanged on a tree." In the story of the crucifixion of Christ we are told that when the even was come, the day the Lord was crucified, the Jews went to the procurator and asked that the crosses be taken down, for the pilgrims were coming into the city for the sacred Passover and the ghastly sight would be offensive to them.

and our salvation, our hope of glory. Christ died. How did He die? Why did He die? Did He die like Socrates, drinking the hemlock, a martyr to philosophical truth? Did He die like Julius Caesar, a hero in the senate before the cruel daggers of Brutus and Cassius? Did He die like the Agamemnon in Aeschylus carrying out the heroic assignment of the Greek nation against the Trojans? Did He die like Shakespeare's tragedy of King Lear? Did He die like Abraham Lincoln under the assassin's bullet in Ford's Theater in Washington? How did He die?

There is a divine meaning in the death of Christ. This is God's plan for our salvation. There is no pardon and peace apart from atonement. There is no remission of sins apart from the shedding of blood and there is no reconciliation without the payment of death. This is our atonement, our propitiation, our sacrifice for sin. This is our means of reconciliation to God. The cross to the Apostle Paul and to us is the same thing as the brazen serpent raised in the wilderness was to Moses and the children of Israel. It is a sign of universal love, mercy, forgiveness, and healing from the hands of God.

> Look and live, my brother, live!
> Look to Jesus now and live;
> 'Tis recorded in His Word, hallelujah!
> It is only that you "look and live."

The cross is a sign of our atonement. It is a sign of our forgiveness. It is a sign of God's inviting love, His invitation to pardon and forgiveness. It is an invitation to life. The cross has an upraised beam. Raised toward the sky, it points toward God in heaven. It has a lower part that touches the earth. God, reaching out His loving hand, extends it down even to us. It has crossarms and they go in either direction as far as the East goes East and as far as the West goes West. The arms of the cross are extended to the limits of the earth. It is the open invitation to all men everywhere to find life, liberty, forgiveness, mercy, and salvation in the atoning love, sobs, tears, suffering death of the Son of God. We are all welcome.

The arms of the cross extend to all mankind—to the Greek

and to the Barbarian, to the Roman and to the provincial, to the Jew and to the Greek, to the bond and to the free, to the lettered and to the unlearned, to the rich and to the poor, to the wise and to the unwise, to the old and to the young, to the near and to those who are far off, to the good and to the not so good, to all of us does God extend wide His invitation. The world could never be the same again because our Lord died in it. It was this planet upon which Jesus spilled His sacred blood.

That cross is a sign of our hope of glory. If there is any tomorrow, if there is any heaven, if there is any God and life yet to be, the cross is a sign of that hope.

> If in Flanders Fields the poppies grow
> It will be between the crosses row to row.

Recently I passed by a large cemetery near Athens, Greece. It was filled with thousands of white crosses. As I looked at them I thought of many other cemeteries, especially American military cemeteries around the world, such as at Arlington, Virginia, in the Philippines, in the Hawaiian Islands, in France. Everywhere above that American boy who has fallen in battle our people erected a cross. Why? Because it is a hope. It is a prayer, it is a vision, it is a dream, it is an expectation, it is a promise, it is an assurance that God has prepared some better thing for us than what we know in the sorrow and tears of this life. If we have any hope, any forgiveness, any tomorrow, it lies in the atoning death of the Son of God.

I was in London one day standing in Charing Cross. Years ago the beloved wife of the King died far away from London. As the King tenderly and lovingly brought her body back to the great city, wherever her body rested in the long journey the King built a little chapel and he called it always by some kind of a cross, as the King's Cross, as Charing Cross. I was standing in Charing Cross in London and a fellow minister by my side said: "Let me tell you a story that happened here. There was a little girl in the city who lost her way. She just wandered around in the streets of London, crying heartbrokenly, pitiously. An English bobby saw the child wandering and stopped her to ask her why her sobbing. The child answered that she was lost and did not know how to find her way home.

The bobby said to her, 'Do not cry. Sit down here by my side and we will find where you live, where home is.' So the bobby sat on the curb of the street and the little broken-hearted girl sat by his side. He said, 'Now I am going to ask you some places in London and you tell me if you recognize any of them. Piccadilly Circus?' 'No.' 'Westminster?' 'No.' 'Charing Cross?' 'Ah,' said the little girl in her tears, 'Yes, yes. Take me down to the cross and I can find my way home from there!' "

How true for all humanity, for all mankind, for our hopes and our hearts, and our lives! Take me to the cross and I can find my way home from there.

I must needs go home
By the way of the cross,
There's no other way but this;
I shall ne'er get sight
Of the gates of light,
If the way of the cross I miss.

I must needs go on
In the blood sprinkled way,
The path that our Saviour trod,
If I ever climb to the heights sublime,
Where my soul is at rest with God.

This is God's invitation to you.

What more can He say
Than to you He hath said,
To you who for refuge
To Jesus have fled?

This is God's love and mercy poured out in the earth. This is God's sweet invitation to us today. Come, come.

CHAPTER 22

SCARS FOR THE LORD

> From henceforth let no man trouble me: for I bear in my body the marks of the Lord Jesus. (Gal. 6:17)

There are two Greek words in the text that immediately command our attention. "For I bear in my body *ta stigmata* of the Lord Jesus." If I could translate them exactly, they would read, "For I bear in my body *the brand marks* of the Lord Jesus."

On the western plains of Texas where I grew up as a boy every ranchman, every bossman, had his brand mark. At the roundups in the spring and in the fall the brand that was on the mother cow was burned into the flesh of the calf. Years ago I went through the heart of Africa. Every native African I saw, unless he was a second-generation Christian, had deep scars cut into the face or somewhere on the body. They were signs that he belonged to a certain clan and a certain tribe.

A similar practice was followed in the days of the Roman Empire. If I could describe the Roman Empire as any one thing above another I would call it an engine of slavery. Out of a population of approximately one hundred million, sixty million were slaves. They were chattel property. If one walked down the streets of Antioch, Ephesus, Athens, Corinth, or Rome in the days when Paul walked down those streets, three men out of every five he met would have been bond slaves. In those days of such massive human servitude the owner cut a scar in the body of the slave in order that his property might be easily identified and apprehended if he ran away. The scar might be in the lobe of the ear, or it might be in the face, or it could be in the hand, or the arm. The Greeks had a name for it, as they proverbially have a name for everything. They called that scar cut in the flesh of the slave a *stigma,* plural *stigmata.* We have taken the word and spelled it the same way, and placed it in our English vocabulary; a "stigma," a sign of shadowed inferiority. But in the days of the Apostle Paul it was the word for the scar cut in the body of the slave, a "stigma." Paul uses that word to describe his own devotion to Christ. "For I bear in my body, *ta stigmata,* the brand marks, the scars of the Lord Jesus."

The Slave of the Lord Jesus

Sometimes the beauty of the language of the King James translation will hide away the rough, jagged edges of the word that the apostle will use. Here is an instance of it. In Romans 1:1; Philippians 1:1; and Titus 1:1, in the King James Version one reads, "Paul, a servant of Jesus Christ." What he actually wrote was *"Paulos doulos Christou Iseou";* that is, "Paul, a *slave* of Jesus Christ." He possessed no life but the life of the Lord. He had no will, no message, no vision, no hope, no tomorrow but that found in Christ Jesus. He was a slave of Jesus Christ, and as a slave he referred to *ta stigamta,* the brand marks, the scars he bore as a sign and symbol of that servitude. He belonged to Jesus.

Deeply do I wish I could have seen the body of the Apostle Paul. His face was covered with scars. I could have asked him, "Paul, what caused those scars?" And he could have replied: "Once was I stoned at Lystra and dragged outside the city for dead. They are the brand marks of the Lord Jesus." I wish I could have seen his back, crossed and crisscrossed with livid scars. "Paul, where did you get those scars?" And he could have replied: "Of the Jews five times received I forty stripes save one, and thrice was I beaten with Roman rods. They are the scars, the brand marks of the Lord Jesus." I wish I could have seen his wrists and his ankles, covered with deep callouses. "Paul, how did you get those callouses?" And he could have replied, "In prison above measure." It is hard for us to realize that most of the ministry of the Apostle Paul was spent in dungeons, manacled in fetters and in stocks.

They are the brand marks, the scars, *ta stigmata,* of the Lord Jesus.

But Paul, are you not boasting, are you not proud of your devotion, are you not lifted up because of your great sufferings for the Lord? No, for he has just written in the text above: "God forbid that I should glory, that I should boast, save in the cross of our Lord Jesus Christ." Well, then, if you are not boasting and glorying in your superlative devotion and illimitable sacrifices, then why, Paul, do you speak of yourself and why do you refer to your scars? The answer is found in the book as a whole. The Book of Galatians was written to the churches he founded on his first missionary journey. As Paul preached he was always followed by Judaizers who said that he was a false apostle, a pseudo-apostle. The real apostles are the Twelve—Peter, James, John, and their fellow disciples. But the Judaizers scornfully said: "This Paul, this Saul, we do not even know how he got into that classification of an apostle. He is not a true emissary from heaven, and the message that he preaches is not the true message of Christ. His gospel is heresy, it is a dilution, it is not a true revelation of the grace of God." Therefore, these enemies spurned his word and discounted his ministry and made little of his efforts. It was in answer to that castigation that Paul wrote this letter called Paul's letter to the churches of Galatia. In defense of his apostleship he writes this text: "For I bear in my body the *stigmata,* the brand marks, the scars of the Lord Jesus."

The Power of the Dedicated Life

Somehow it is most difficult to scorn, to ridicule, and to belittle real devotion, the pouring out of life unto death. I remember one time seeing on the front page of the *Dallas Morning News* the picture of a minister of the Birtish government as he stood before a student group of the University of Glasgow. He was a strange-looking spectacle because the students who evidently disliked the British government at that time and especially that particular representative of it, had come prepared for him. When he was introduced and stood there on the platform, they pelted him with rotten eggs, rotten vegetables and finally with flour. As I looked at the picture of the insults they planned and executed on that minister of the British government, my mind went back to another occasion when in that same university another man had been introduced to the student group. The chancellor of the university that day introduced to the young men of the University of Glasgow God's missionary, David Livingstone. In the history book that I read it said that when David Livingstone stood up and walked to the front of the dais to speak to the group, the students looked at him earnestly. They saw his hair burned crisp under the torrid, tropical sun. They saw his body wasted and emaciated with jungle fever. They saw his right arm hanging limp at his side, destroyed by the attack of a ferocious African lion. And the book said that when the students looked at him they stood up with one accord in awe and in silence before God's missionary. There is a power in consecration and devotion that grips the human heart and it is difficult to belittle it or ridicule it.

Is that not the power of the Son of God? The message that saves us from our sins, is it not the story of the cross, the message of His sufferings, the preaching of His love and life poured out unto death? If there had been no Gethsemane, and had there been no cross, and no crown of thorns, and no blood poured out, we would yet be in our sins. The power of the Gospel of Christ is found in His suffering and in His cross. Inevitably the corollary and concomitant is no less true. The power of the church has always been in its consecration and in its devotion—in the blood of the martyrs, in the songs of those who praised God while they were being burned at the stake, in the pouring out of life unto death in behalf of the name of Christ—the *stigmata*, the scars of the Lord.

There is another addendum that follows. The weakness of the church is found in its lack of devotion—our unburdened hearts, our unprayed prayers, our unspoken testimonies, our unoffered gifts. We give something if there is anything left over, if it does not cost us anything. We come if it is convenient. But as for the pouring out of life unto death, as for tears of intercession and burden, as for consecration that God can use and bless, we hardly know it in our effete and effeminate life of ease.

I remember when I was in Oberammergau looking at that

famous Passion Play. I was told that in a previous time there was an American tourist and his wife who were there in attendance at the play. Between acts the wife of the American tourist said to her husband, "Now you pick up that cross and I will take a picture of you carrying the cross." He thought it was a good idea so he walked over to pick up the cross while his wife took a picture of him. He could not even lift it. About that time Anthony Lang came by, the great man who for thirty years played the part of the Christus in the play. The American asked him: "Why so heavy? This is just a play. This is just an act. Why is the cross so heavy?" Anthony Lang humbly and simply answered, "Sir, when I carry it, if I do not feel it, I cannot play my part."

It is thus with our devotion to Christ. If it does not cost me anything, if I do not feel it, it becomes meaningless. And that is exactly the measure of our devotion before God. If it costs us nothing then it turns to dust and ashes in our hands. The power of the testimony and the reality of the message are defined by the tears, sobs, prayers, and sacrifice that we are willing to pour into it. If there are no tears, and if there is no sacrifice, and if it does not cost, then the witness is feeble, sterile, and empty in the earth. Where are our scars for the Lord?

The Call of God for the Sacrificial Work of Witnessing

Oh, to call our church to a tremendous dedication! Would God we did our secular work to make a living, to pay the bills, but actually our lives are God's and what we do we do for the glory of the Lord. Of all the things in this ultimate devotion concerning which I could speak, pouring our lives into the service of Christ, I choose one to discuss. It is the main one, the one that colors all others. It is the devotion that leads us to win lost people to Jesus, to search for them, to pray for them, to witness to them, to bring them to the Lord. That is our primary mandate.

Something happened when I was a youth, just beginning to preach, that gave a color and an emphasis to every day of my Gospel ministry through the years since. One time through a friend I accepted an invitation to preach in a two-week revival meeting in a place I had never seen, in a church of which I had never heard and with a pastor I did not know. For two weeks I preached to that little country congregation. There was no burden, there was no prayer of agony for the lost, there was no effort to win anyone to Christ. For two weeks every morning and every night I held that revival meeting and the effort was barren, sterile, empty, and void. At the Friday morning service of the second week I went through the congregation and asked them one at a time: "Do you have a burden for the lost? Is there someone you are praying to be saved? Is there someone whom you lay before God's throne of saving grace? Is there someone on your heart?" I went through the entire congregation and the answer was "No." There was nobody burdened for anyone. I was ready to dismiss the service in despair. The whole revival was a daily Gethsemane to me. I just died and suffered in my soul. But before the benediction that Friday morning, a little mother on the second row at the end of the seat held up her hand and said: "Brother Criswell, wait, wait. My husband died several years ago. I am a widow and I have two boys. I am trying to raise those two boys. My boys are lost." She broke down and cried, repeating the words, "My two boys are lost." When she could gain her composure she added, "Oh, that someone would help me win my two boys to Christ!"

After the service was over we went to a beautiful Kentucky home such as you think of in that Blue Grass State. There was a lovely dinner prepared by the hostess of the home. The table groaned under the vittles that were cooked and placed on the table. After all of us had eaten to our hearts' content we went outside on the beautiful lawn in front of the home and sat down under the graceful maple trees. We were talking and talking and the afternoon was slipping away. My heart grew increasingly heavy. I moved my chair over by the side of the pastor's and I said to him, "Did you hear that little woman this morning?" He said, "Yes." "Her two boys are lost?" He said, "Yes." 'And did you hear her plea that someone would help win them to Jesus?" He said, "Yes." I then asked, "What are you going to do about it?" And he replied: "Why, nothing. If God wants those boys saved He will save them without your help or mine." I found out that the whole church was like that. "God is going to do it; we are not going to do anything." I said to him, "Could I be excused from this lovely and gracious company, and would someone take me to that little mother's house?" He said, "Why, certainly, if you want to go." I said, "I want to go there more than anything in the world." So I excused myself from the lovely company, got in a car, and a man took me to the lane where she lived. I got out of the car and I said, "I'll get to the church somehow tonight."

It was thus that I walked up that lane and knocked at the humble farm home. That little mother came to the door. I said: "Mother, I heard what you said this morning. Your two boys are lost. Where are those boys?" She replied, "My younger son is in the barn milking the cows, and my older son has not come in yet from the fields." I asked, "Mother, would you get down on your knees and stay on your knees and pray and ask God as I try to win those boys to Jesus?" She said, "I will." And she got down on her knees to pray. I went out to the barn. There was the younger boy about sixteen years old milking the cows. I sat down on a box by the side of the stool on which he was seated milking the cows and I said to him, "Son, your mother is inside the house on her knees praying for you." I then opened my little New Testament and said, "I want to read to you out of God's Book how to be saved." I read him those passages in God's Book that tell us how to be saved and then I asked, "Son, would you kneel down here by my side and pray with me?" He stopped his milking and knelt down by my side. I put my arm around him, and prayed for him that God would save him. When I finished the prayer I extended my hand and said, "Son, if you will give your heart to Jesus, take my hand." He squeezed it hard, saying, "I will take the Lord as my Savior."

By that time the older boy had come in from the fields and was taking the harness off of the horses and hanging it on pegs in the barn. I went up to him and said, "Son, your mother is inside the house on her knees praying for you, and I want to read to you out of God's book how a boy can be saved." I read to him those precious passages and then I asked, "Son, would you get down here on your knees by my side?"

He knelt by my side and I prayed that God would save him. When I finished the prayer I extended my hand, on our knees, and I said, "Son, if you will take the Lord as your Savior, will you grasp my hand?" And he nearly crushed my hand, he held it so hard.

That night at church when I gave the invitation those two boys came forward, arm in arm. It was a glorious sight, and that sweet mother shouted. I have not heard anyone shout in thirty years. She shouted that night. Those two boys were the only boys, the only people, the only souls that were saved in the meeting. When it was finished I went away with a commitment and a resolution in my heart that has colored my ministry ever since. I believe that the praying, the working, and the dedication of the whole church ought to be to one holy and heavenly end, namely, that the lost may come to know God. That is what it is all about. If we are teaching, we are teaching toward that goal. If we are reaching and striving, we are striving toward that goal. If we are living and talking, we are living and talking for that purpose. Somehow God will bless the words we say, and the life we live, and the deeds we do, that the lost might be saved.

Recently a discerning visitor said to me, "I love to come to Dallas to go to the First Baptist Church because when I sit there in the services I know that when the invitation is extended God is going to give a harvest." And he said, "It blesses my heart more than anything in the service to see people coming down that aisle, taking Jesus as Savior." I said to him: "Sir, I am exactly like you. As glorious as a choir can sing, and as marvelous as is the spirit of the congregation in loving to be together and praising God, the sweetest and the most meaningful thing we do is to see people come out of that balcony, come out of the pews in the lower floor and into the aisles down here to the front, giving their lives to the blessed Jesus."

The strength of our witness, the measure of our devotion, the power of our appeal, lies in the blood, tears, sacrifice, dedication, toil, and sweat we are willing to pour into it. Where are our scars for the Lord? "For I bear in my body the scars, the brand marks, the *stigmata*, of the Lord Jesus."